SOCIAL AREA ANALYSIS

Stanford Sociological Series

NUMBER ONE

SOCIAL AREA ANALYSIS,

Theory, Illustrative Application and Computational Procedures

By

ESHREF SHEVKY and WENDELL BELL

GREENWOOD PRESS, PUBLISHERS
WESTPORT, CONNECTICUT

The Library of Congress has catalogued this publication as follows:

Library of Congress Cataloging in Publication Data

Shevky, Eshref.
    Social area analysis.

    Original ed. issued as no. 1 of Stanford sociological
series.
    Bibliography: p.
    1. Social surveys. 2. Social surveys--San
Francisco Bay region. 3. San Francisco Bay region--
Social conditions. I. Bell, Wendell, joint author.
II. Title.
[HN29.S5 1972]   309.1'794'6   75-147222
ISBN 0-8371-5987-3

This study was made possible by funds granted by Carnegie Corporation of New York. That Corporation is not, however, the author, owner, publisher, or proprietor of this publication, and is not to be understood as approving by virtue of its grant any of the statements made or views expressed therein.

Originally published in 1955 by Stanford University Press, Stanford, California

Reprinted by arrangement with Stanford University Press

Reprinted by Greenwood Press, Inc.

First Greenwood reprinting 1972
Second Greenwood reprinting 1973
Third Greenwood reprinting 1977

Library of Congress catalog card number 75-147222

ISBN 0-8371-5987-3

Printed in the United States of America

ACKNOWLEDGMENTS

The method of urban analysis presented here is based on work which has received financial support from various sources. The Haynes Foundation supported the original work which was reported in *The Social Areas of Los Angeles* (1949). Continued exploration in the utility and application of the method was conducted with the support of the Social Science Research Council through the Pacific Coast Committee on Community Studies and through a Predoctoral Research Training Fellowship which was awarded to Wendell Bell in 1951–52. For the analysis of empirical materials and the statement of the method which appear in this volume we are indebted to the Carnegie Corporation of New York and the Stanford Committee for Research in the Social Sciences. To each of the above we wish to express our gratitude.

The many discussions with the members of the SSRC Pacific Coast Committee on Community Studies were very helpful in the clarification of our underlying theory and in the solution of methodological problems. We are particularly indebted to Professors Harold E. Jones (University of California, Berkeley), under whose sponsorship the committee was formed, Leonard Broom (University of California, Los Angeles), William S. Robinson (University of California, Los Angeles), Calvin F. Schmid (University of Washington), and Robert C. Tryon (University of California, Berkeley).

For his careful reading of the manuscript and his valuable suggestions concerning form and style we wish to thank Professor Paul Wallin (Stanford University). Discussions and joint work with Professor Scott Greer (Occidental College) and Mr. Channing Murray (University of California, Los Angeles) have contributed importantly to the organization of Chapter II. We thank Mr. Marion D. Boat (Stanford University) and Mrs. Maryanne T. Force (Stanford University) for their careful work in the performance of the necessary statistical calculations.

E. S.
W. B.

UNIVERSITY OF CALIFORNIA, LOS ANGELES
and
STANFORD UNIVERSITY

v

TABLE OF CONTENTS

I. INTRODUCTION

The investigations summarized here had as their point of departure the detailed knowledge of the structure of urban areas derived from the studies of urban ecologists, and the contributions of those geographers and economists who have concerned themselves with problems of urban structure and function. The techniques we have used have grown out of the experience of many of these studies in handling small area statistics. Not a few of the judgments that guided the initial development of the urban typology described here were tested by the inspection of the detailed ecological maps of Columbus, Chicago, St. Louis, Minneapolis–St. Paul, Seattle, and other urban areas, which we owe to such men as McKenzie (1923), Zorbaugh (1929), Queen (1935), and Schmid (1937, 1944). Beyond this point, however, our concern with problems of social differentiation and stratification has led us to a different kind of analysis, and our attention has been focused on relationships of a different order than those considered by urban ecologists.

The original formulation of this method was the result of an assignment to study the urban phenomena of Los Angeles in the context of the "community." It appeared at the outset, however, that the use of existing models for community research would leave many unresolved problems of method and, in the end, this large urban aggregate, Los Angeles, would have to be considered either "unique," or "not a city at all."

Rather than accept such a conclusion, it was thought more useful to revise the model for the study, and the terms of reference of the project were altered by proceeding on the assumption that the urban phenomena of Los Angeles were regional manifestations of changes in the total society, and the further assumption that, in urban analysis, facts of economic differentiation and of status and power had a significance transcending in importance the significance of relations occurring within the boundaries of the local community. It was observed that the sociologists who considered the spatial patterning discovered in the city as the "basic underpinning" for the study of urban life ran the risk of becoming bounded by the particularities of the urban frame taken in isolation. The objective of the Los Angeles study, however, was to understand urban aggregations, not as isolated, self-contained units, but as parts of a wider system of relationships. The choice was made to deal with the social statistics of very large cities, not because of a belief that these cities were independent, "dominant" factors, but because of the conviction that the emerging characteristics of modern society were best observed in such areas of movement and expansion.

The implications of this orientation for the study of contemporary, large, urban aggregations have been stated by Shevky and Williams (1949) and by Bell (1952). The present joint contribution aims to accomplish two major purposes. The first is *to restate the basic orientation and to specify the steps in the construct formation and index construction of this method of urban analysis.* Shevky and Williams' initial formulation was preceded by a long-term effort to achieve an integration of relevant theory with empirical aspects of the trend of urban differentiation in modern industrial society. For purposes of brevity and sharpness of focus, their formulation is now presented in propositional form, without any attempt to do justice to the enormous complexity of the matters discussed. We reconsider and restate the concept, urbanization, as originally developed in the Los Angeles study, and specify the more limited but important meaning we now attach to the index of urbanization as originally constructed. Chapter II is devoted to this restatement and specification, and within the limits of the specific aspects of theory dealt with, this part of our paper constitutes for us a major step in theory construction and marks out for us one direction of future work.

The second major purpose of this monograph is *to demonstrate the use of the typology as an analytic framework for the comparative study of certain aspects of the social structure of American cities.* We feel that the application of this typology to census and comparable data available for American cities will allow the beginning of the systematic accumulation of knowledge about the social organization, especially the stratification and differentiation, of American urban populations.

While further refinements will no doubt be made, the modifications in the typology given in Chapter IV will permit its use in comparative urban analysis wherever census tract statistics are available. Chapter V contains an illustration of the application of the typology in a comparative framework to a set of empirical data, and Chapter VI gives a step-by-step statement of the computational procedures. These last two chapters, taken together, are designed as an illustrative workbook for other research workers who may wish to use the typology in other cities.

Chapter III, although brief, is included to emphasize the fact that the empirical case presented in Chapter V represents only one of the many uses to which the general method can be put.

II. CONSTRUCT FORMATION AND THE FRAMEWORK OF SOCIAL TRENDS

AN OVERVIEW

The urban typology of *The Social Areas of Los Angeles* (1949) is a classificatory schema designed to categorize census tract populations in terms of three basic factors—social rank, urbanization, and segregation. Each census tract population was given three scores, one for each of the indexes of the factors; and then the tract populations with similar configurations of scores on the three indexes were grouped together into larger units called social areas. We begin the restatement of our theoretical orientation by sketching out the reasoning which led to the development of the constructs of social rank, urbanization, and segregation as basic factors in the social differentiation and stratification of the contemporary city. Although an elaboration follows in the remainder of Chapter II, the chief elements of our argument have been laid out in schematic form in Table II-1. The arrows in the table indicate the direction of our reasoning. These trends, of course, are interrelated, but their interconnections are not indicated in the table.

We conceive of the city as a product of the complex whole of modern society; thus the social forms of urban life are to be understood within the context of the changing character of the larger containing society. In Column 1 of Table II-1 we have given some statements descriptive of modern society as compared with traditional societies, or of a particular modern society compared at two points in time. These we call "postulates concerning industrial society" and they each are aspects of the increasing scale of modern society. As descriptive statements, or broad postulates, their analytic utility is not very great. Their utility increases, however, to the extent that we can identify the modes of organization associated with them.

In Column 2 of Table II-1 we make such an identification. Three broad sets of interrelated trends are specified: these are changes in (1) the distribution of skills, (2) the organization of productive activity, and (3) the composition of the population. These three trends appear to be most descriptive of the changing character of modern society. At particular points in time, given social systems can be conceived as standing in differential relationships to these three major trends. As illustrative of these trends, three sets of changes are given in Column 3 of Table II-1. These are changes in the arrangement of occupations, changes in the ways of living, and redistribution of the population in space. The trends are here seen as specific changes in the structure of a given social system.

However, subpopulations in a particular society at a given point in time also can be conceived as standing in differential relationships to these three sets of structural changes. In Column 4 of Table II-1 the three sets of structural changes in a given social system (Column 3) have been redefined as *structural reflections* of change to serve as descriptive and analytic concepts for the study of modern social structure. Thus, from certain broad postulates concerning modern society and from the analysis of temporal trends, we have selected three structural reflections of change which can be used as factors for the study of

3

TABLE II-1
STEPS IN CONSTRUCT FORMATION AND INDEX CONSTRUCTION

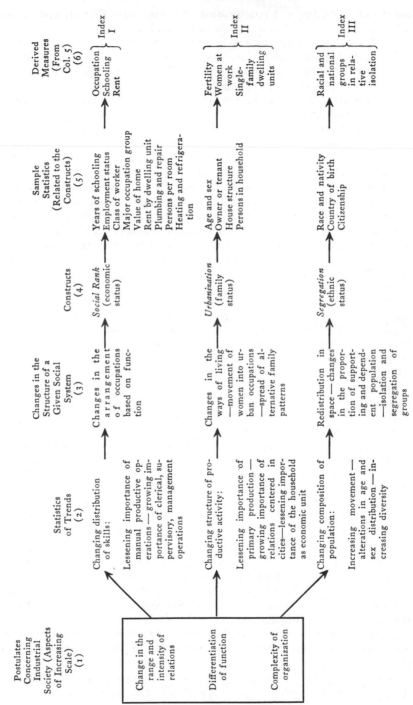

social differentiation and stratification at a particular time in modern society. These factors are social rank, urbanization, and segregation.[1]

The next step in the construction of the urban typology is to select indexes of the three factors. Sample statistics related to the constructs and available for urban analysis are listed in Column 5 of Table II-1. These categories represent those given in the 1940 census bulletins for population and housing statistics by census tracts. With the constructs designated and the elements of each of the three major social trends specified, it was a simple matter to group the census variables into three groups according to the constructs to which they were most related. Certain of these census variables are more direct measures of the constructs than the others and are more useful as measures of the three factors. The variables selected to compose the indexes of social rank, urbanization, and segregation are indicated in Column 6 of Table II-1. These derived measures indicate aspects of urban population which are most clearly indicative of the changing distribution of skills, the changing organization of productive activity (especially the changing structure of the family), and the changing composition of the population. Before presenting the illustrative analysis of the social differentiation of the San Francisco Bay Region as of 1940 and 1950, using the three indexes, we will elaborate further on the analysis of trends and the construct formation just presented in schematic form.

THE FRAMEWORK OF SOCIAL TRENDS

The primitive idea of scale.—The course of economic development in industrial societies is reflected in Colin Clark's (1951) data on real income per man-hours worked as measured in his "international units." The work of this investigator, extending over more than a decade, has given us insight into the changes in the structure of productive activity which have accompanied growth in industrial society.

The fundamental generalization that emerges from Clark's investigation is that modern economies tend to move toward more complex organization and higher income levels in a series of steps: first, the intensification of *primary* production, agriculture, forestry, and mining; second, the expansion of *secondary* production, manufacturing, and construction; third, the proportionally greater expansion of *tertiary* production, trade, transportation, communication, and services. As Clark (1951) points out in his *Conditions of Economic Progress*, we can draw the above conclusions either from an examination of the present situation in different countries, or different parts of the same country, or from examining figures for each country over a series of years.

In low-income, industrially less advanced countries, an overwhelming proportion of the working population is concentrated in primary production. With each succeeding step in industrial development, the population in secondary and tertiary production increases until levels observed in Britain, the United States, and Australia are achieved.

The nature of the occupational structure in economies such as these, and their remarkable similarity, is apparent in the summary description given in Table II-2.

---

[1] Note the alternative designations in Column 4 of Table II-1 given for the three factors. See Appendix C for two views of the constructs briefly stated.

TABLE II-2

INDUSTRIAL STRUCTURE: PERCENTAGE OF ALL WORKERS ENGAGED IN
MAIN ORDERS OF TRANSACTIONS IN BRITAIN AND AMERICA*

	U.S.A. Census of 1940	England and Wales Census of 1931
Agriculture and fishing	18.8	6.0
Mining and quarrying, wells	2.0	5.9
Manufacture	23.4	32.1
Public utilities	1.2	1.2
Building	4.6	5.1
Services	48.5	49.5
Not classified	1.5	.2
Total	100.0	100.0

* Adapted from Florence (1953: 5).

Comparable data for the United States through time, for various national economies, and for various states within the Union show the same trends.

The proportion of the work force in secondary occupations (manufacturing) has grown only slightly in the United States since 1910, but as Florence (1953:6) reminds us, in man *plus* mechanical power productivity of the work force has grown greatly.

The mechanization of industry is indeed the main cause of the relative stability of the working force in manufacture compared to services, and not, as some would have it, national maturity or even decadence. The use of machines allows more output to be made with the same number of human producers and results in more man-power for selling and distribution services which cannot so easily be mechanized. Another cause for the relative advance of services is higher standards of living; as communities get richer more of their income tends to be spent on such services as restaurants, travel and hotels, education, medical attention; and government services, too, tend to increase.

Furthermore, as Florence notes in another connection, and as Arthur Salz (1937) has made specific, the increasingly complex industrial culture of machines forces a growing administrative personnel, much of which is not identified with manufacturing.

The progressive displacement of workers from primary to secondary, finally to tertiary, occupations is thus to be understood as a continuing dynamic—the stability of manpower in manufacturing notwithstanding. There are indications today that mechanization is gradually moving into those areas regarded less amenable to the machine; as C. Wright Mills (1951) points out, the retail service workers are increasingly confronting the threat of the automat, and Norbert Wiener (1950) has noted that a large part of the white-collar clerical work is easily performed by electronic equipment.

Briefly stated, the substitution of machines for men in the secondary (and more slowly in the primary) occupations releases an increasingly larger population for tertiary occupations. This is concomitant with an increase in wealth which allows for a wider range of social choices both in the investment of time and the distribution of the surplus. Little data are available on the social and cultural implications of this, but certainly they are crucial for a study of urban life.

The rapid urbanization of the United States during the last one hundred years was made possible, then, by the transfer of workers from agriculture to manufacture and trade. Shifts in the character of economic opportunity, brought about by increasing urbanization and industrialization, caused changes in the regional distribution of workers, resulted in regional specialization and local differentiation, and produced population movements and mixtures having wide and ramified consequences.

These were aspects of an increase in the *scale of the society*.[2] If we conceive of scale as the scope of social interaction and dependency, the past century has witnessed a vast increase in the scale of American society. Not only has the total national population become more interdependent, with a resulting increase in the scope of interaction—but American society has relations with most of the people of the earth. At the same time, the intensity of dependence on and interaction with the immediate social environment has tended to diminish: "national consciousness," in general, becomes more important, "neighborhood consciousness" less so. Such an increase in scale, however, also has the effect of increasing the heterogeneity of the populations included in the same society. The society which is large in scale must, of necessity, encompass many local variations—economic, ethnic, regional, and the like.

One of the few germinal papers which attempts to describe and account for the effects of increasing scale in society is that of Louis Wirth (1938). His postulates and his argument can be summarized as follows:

LOUIS WIRTH'S SOCIOLOGICAL DEFINITION OF THE CITY IN RELATION TO SIZE, DENSITY, AND HETEROGENEITY

A SCHEMATIC VERSION

Size	
An increase in the number of inhabitants of a settlement beyond a certain limit brings about changes in the relations of people and changes in the character of the community	Greater the number of people interacting, greater the potential differentiation
	Dependence upon a greater number of people, lesser dependence on particular persons
	Association with more people, knowledge of a smaller proportion, and of these, less intimate knowledge
	More secondary rather than primary contacts; that is, increase in contacts which are face to face, yet impersonal, superficial, transitory, and segmental
	More freedom from the personal and emotional control of intimate groups
	Association in a large number of groups, no individual allegiance to a single group

[2] The particular use we make of the postulate of scale derives directly from the work of two social anthropologists, the late Godfrey Wilson and Monica Wilson (1945).

Density

Reinforces the effect of size in diversifying men and their activities, and in increasing the structural complexity of the society

{
Tendency to differentiation and specialization

Separation of residence from work place

Functional specialization of areas—segregation of functions

Segregation of people: city becomes a mosaic of social worlds
}

Heterogeneity

Cities products of migration of peoples of diverse origin

Heterogeneity of origin matched by heterogeneity of occupations

Differentiation and specialization reinforces heterogeneity

{
Without common background and common activities premium is placed on visual recognition: the uniform becomes symbolic of the role

No common set of values, no common ethical system to sustain them: money tends to become measure of all things for which there are no common standards

Formal controls as opposed to informal controls. Necessity for adhering to predictable routines. Clock and the traffic signal symbolic of the basis of the social order

Economic basis: mass production of goods, possible only with the standardization of processes and products

Standardization of goods and facilities in terms of the average

Adjustment of educational, recreational, and cultural services to mass requirements

In politics success of mass appeals—growth of mass movements
}

Wirth's analysis, valuable as it is in calling attention to the specific attributes of modern society as distinguished from traditional, agrarian societies, is nevertheless incomplete in its underlying assumption: *it is not the city which is an underlying "prime mover" in the recent transformation of Western society, but the necessities of economic expansion itself.* Size, density, and heterogeneity, important in describing the urban ambit, are not the most significant *structural* aspects of urbanization—for urbanization is a state of a total society, as well as of its cities.

It is our contention that the postulate of increasing scale in modern society gains in analytic utility when we are able to specify that in *all technologically advanced modern societies* the most important concomitant of changes in productivity, and changes in economic organization with the consequent alterations of

They discuss the problem of increasing scale in modern central Africa. We attempt to relate certain aspects of this concept to the trend of development in Western society.

social relations, has been the movement of working population from agriculture to manufacture, and from manufacture to commerce, communication, transport, and service.[3]

The nature of the transformation subsumed under this trend has indeed been far-reaching, for in the course of this change:

1. The existing forms of income-producing property became altered.

2. The growth curve of population changed.

3. Urban aggregates increased by both (a) "multiplication of points of concentration, and (b) the growth of individual concentrations."

4. Demographic changes accompanied urbanization and the shift from a rural household to an urban industrial economy.

5. The nature of enterprise changed.

6. A large and growing body of salaried and wage-earning employees came into existence.

7. The nature of the professions changed—in relation to them there developed a large body of semiprofessional workers.

8. There developed in conspicuous importance a body of managerial and supervisory personnel, occupying positions of co-ordination, control, and direction.

Clark's generalization, thus, provides us with a set of structural indicators with which to approach the problem of increasing scale. We distinguish three broad and interrelated trends associated with three orders of organizational complexity: changes in the distribution of skills, changes in the structure of productive activity, and changes in the composition of population.

Changes in the distribution of skills.—The first trend is the change in the distribution of skills. *As societies increase in scale, the nature of income-producing property is altered; land gives way to the enterprise, and ownership of the enterprise becomes less significant than position within a given enterprise. At the same time, the occupations within a society are regrouped: they become hierarchically organized into levels of skill, income, and prestige.*

Modern society, in contradistinction to traditional societies, is organized on an occupational basis. Only in the modern period has occupation come to have a determining influence upon status and rank; today, no other single characteristic tells us so much about the individual and his position in society.

The key significance of occupation stems from its many connotations; from its technological and economic meaning, as well as from its social meaning. The *technological* meaning is significant because occupation is equated with specific mental and manual operations involved in work, the *economic* meaning in that occupations are related to given levels of income, and the *social* meaning because a person or his group achieves status and rank by virtue of his occupation (Salz, 1937). In fact, the historic association of property with power becomes altered, and power tends to derive increasingly from positions in functioning organizations—that is, occupations. The generality of the occupation as a determinant

---

[3] For a social anthropological perspective on the study of the process of urbanization, see Beals (1951).

of social position in America has been well documented. High positive correlations have been found between occupation and income, between occupation and education, between occupation and prestige, and between occupation and subjective placements.

Just as occupation has so much meaning in regard to individual position or rank, no single set of closely related facts tell us so much about a total society as do the statistics describing its working population. The manner in which the work force is distributed among the larger groupings of occupations, the proportion they bear to one another, is significantly related to the economic organization, the level of living of the society, and the class system of that society.

Changes in the structure of productive activity.—The second trend is reflected in the changes in the structure of productive activity. *As societies increase in scale, the structure of productive activity changes. The relation of the population to its food supply becomes altered. Primary production declines in importance. The range of relations centered in cities increases. The family loses its specifically economic, productive functions.*

We distinguish three phases of this aspect: (1) the relation of population to the economy; (2) the range of relations centered in cities; and (3) changes in the function and structure of the family. These are the three phases of the primitive notion of *urbanization* as we intend to use it.

1. The first important phase of urbanization is the relation of the population to the economy. Here we rely upon the analysis of Theodore W. Schultz (1953).

We have been aware of the utility of the notion of demographic types in population analysis for some time; the scheme of Notestein (1945), for example, with three types of population, has been particularly useful. Notestein posits one demographic type in which birth and death rates are both high, yielding a constant population; a second type, in which the death rate drops rapidly and the birth rate more slowly, yielding a rapidly expanding population; and a third type in which the birth rate keeps dropping while the death rate reaches a minimum, the rate of increase slows down, and population stability at a new level, or even decrease, is possible.

Such a scheme tells us little, however, concerning the relationship between population fluctuation and outside variables. It is here that Schultz's typology is valuable. Schultz (1953) postulates a dichotomy of populations, as follows:

a) Changes in the population can be explained, at least in large part, as a (within) variable dependent upon the food economy, that is, the population behaves like an endogenous variable of the economic system.

b) Changes in population are determined by circumstances that appear to be outside the economic system, population behaves like an exogenous variable, although it does, of course, affect the economy in many ways.

In Schultz's first type of population, the stable value system would operate to breed the human population up to the maximum possible. This being true, the maximum possible would *determine* population. Empirically, such populations are characterized by high birth and death rates—as in Notestein's scheme.

When, however, there is a change in the value system, for whatever reason, affecting the human breeding rate, it is possible for the food economy to outstrip the population. As this occurs, the population becomes less and less a "within" variable. It is in transition. In such a society the death rate will drop, and we will find an expanding population (though not necessarily a wealthy one). This corresponds to Notestein's second type.

The third type of society is one that is freed from the food determinant. In Schultz's words, "As the level of living rises and the proportion of income spent for the farm-produced services in food falls, there comes a point where changes in the population cannot be explained by what happens in the agricultural sector of the economy" (1953: 35).

Empirically, we should note that the least industrialized nations fall in the first type, the rapidly industrializing nations in the second type, while the more industrialized nations such as the United States and Britain fall in the third type.

Schultz's explanatory theory may be compared with Jaffe's (1940) statistics on fertility in early America; Jaffe shows that long before the intense industrialism of the nineteenth century the variations in birth rates were as extreme within the society as they are today. In every case, the more urban eastern seaboard had lower fertility rates.[4]

To explain the variation in birth rates in communities at similar industrial levels, Schultz advances a hypothesis that the preference for children (familism) or the preference for property (mobility) may have a particular substitution rate —and a multitude of choices would produce the variations. What are the preconditions for this range of preference?

As societies increase in scale the web of organization allows for more protection against famine—trade alone becomes of great importance in this connection. It is likely that the principal drops in the death rate to date have been due to food supply, not medicine. At the same time, the increase in population tends to produce urban concentration. When such an urban concentration in turn stimulates an increase in agricultural production for the urban market, the dynamic has commenced which will transform the society.[5] Two things happen: first, continual changes in the structure of production, creating new channels of social mobility, and second, increased food. These in turn allow alternatives at the individual and group level, between family and occupational mobility. In a sense the individual still has the choice of breeding up to the food supply, or investing in property, career, etc. It is possible that, once a society has gone "outside" the Malthusian limits, variations in population will be an expression of a wide range of alternatives for individuals.

Thus the process of urbanization need not be seen as a process necessarily leading to a declining population; no known society which retained its organization has ever had a violent negative drop in population[6]—this occurs only in the

---

[4] See also the statistical evidence on the marriage pattern of Western Europe cited by Hajnal (1953).

[5] This is an oversimplified statement of a complex phenomenon. We make no effort to specify the conditions under which it occurs. For an illuminating discussion of necessary conditions for the basic development, see Spengler (1951: 21–24).

[6] On this point consult Lotka (1925: 70).

event of catastrophe. Instead of seeing the urban process as inevitably producing lower birth rates, growing in intensity with increased "exposure" of the population to the process, we prefer to suggest that relatively fixed preference alternatives may exist within the framework of modern society. Since the pressure of the population on the food supply no longer explains population growth in such societies as the United States, other explanatory concepts are needed. We would follow Schultz's hypothesis and postulate a range of available choices including, at least, familism, vertical social mobility, and consumption.

2. The second aspect of the primitive notion of urbanization is the great change in the *range of social relations* centered in cities. Here we have specific reference to the centralization of (*a*) the functions of co-ordination and control, (*b*) the service functions, and (*c*) the functions of promotion and innovation.

Occupational changes we take to be indicators of this trend have been documented by Fisher (1939) for Australia and New Zealand, and by Clark (1951) for many countries of the world. The centralization of the co-ordinating functions as a necessity of large-scale organization has been analyzed and discussed in some detail for the New York Region by Haig (1926); Clark (1945) has provided detailed comparative material documenting the fact that under modern conditions the principal function of cities has come to be, not the production of goods, but the provision of services.

This centralization of the co-ordinating functions is an aspect of the concept of *metropolitan dominance* in the formulations of urban ecologists. The currency of the concept arises out of the convergence of a wide range of empirical observations, and the results of many geographic, historical, and economic studies. The *concentration of retail trade*, and the *deconcentration of manufacturing*, in the more recent terminology of the urban ecologists, also refer to tendencies associated with the same phenomena.

Our emphasis, however, falls not on the concentration of retail services, but upon the centralization of the functions of co-ordination, control, and promotion, as an aspect of large-scale organization, for we believe this to be of much greater sociological significance.

All of these functions may be seen today in the centralization of the functions of private and public government in cities, but when we review the historical origins of the city we are made cognizant of the consistent and dominating importance of the control and service functions. Pirenne (1925) dates the rise of certain medieval cities from the origin of the market—and as the market grew in importance and became a system of control, control became centered in the city.

We should see the city, then, as dominant always in relation to a system of interaction, interdependence, and control which embraces the total society. So today, as the "free market" ceases to be the major type of control system and its place is taken by formal (public and private) governmental functions, these relations remain centered in the cities. As society increases in scale it ceases to be organized chiefly in autonomous local units and becomes organized in terms of a far-reaching web or organization, whose points of convergence are typically urban. Such a system is necessarily one of large, extended organizations—

and a dwindling proportion of individuals is required for the control positions.[7]

At the same time, however, primary production absorbs less and less of the available labor force, the surplus going into the occupational stratum *between* manual labor and positions of control. So in every modern socioeconomic system we find the phenomenon of a rapidly increasing "new middle class," or white-collar class. This class processes and communicates order; it provides services; it monopolizes relations with the customer. The growth of this class is clearly recognized as a new social dynamic in the social order in the analyses of Salz (1937) and Mills (1951), among others. It is our contention that such a class is an inevitable concomitant of expanding industrial societies, a persistent characteristic of urbanized organization.

3. Change in the economic functions of the family is a third important phase of urbanization. From the early work of Ogburn (1933) until the present, all available evidence indicates very clearly that the household becomes less and less important as a center of production when societies increase in scale. The family which, in traditional agrarian societies, carried the functions of economic production, distribution, and consumption—as well as those of status ascription, kinship, and many others—is today dependent upon other organizational modes for most of these functions.

As the economic functions are separated from the kinship functions of the family, the kinship functions change in importance and definition. In essence, the size and nature of the conjugal family become variables *related to* (but not determined by) occupation, the latter being a function of large extended organizations beyond the control of the individual.

The relation of conjugal family to occupation, in turn, gives rise to specific variations in family size. The relation between occupational *level* and family size was until recently firmly established. However, recent data indicate an increase in family size in upper-level occupations, and a decrease in lower levels of the hierarchy. In view of variations in size of family within the same occupational levels, we suggest two separate processes: (*a*) certain populations within the city are in process of transition from large families to small families, and (*b*) there is, in a society freed from the Malthusian determinants, an ongoing differentiating process producing *relatively fixed alternative forms of family* ranged on a scale of preference. Adoption of a given family form by a community would be, then, the result of other factors than the existence of economic surplus; it would be explicable only with reference to value systems and ranges of choice.

There are certain functional interrelations between these aspects of urbanization which should be stated. Interconnected changes take place in a society experiencing increase in scale. Important examples are (1) the isolation of the conjugal family, (2) the changed position of women, including the movement of women into urban occupations, and (3) changes in the style of life and the ways of living.

Talcott Parsons (1943) has analyzed the functional importance of the isolated conjugal family for a society which is based upon *free labor*—one in which

[7] On this point compare Greer's discussion (1954).

the individual is selectively attached to one out of many occupational structures. Such isolation, however, also has the effect of weakening certain constraints which tend to preserve the conjugal relationship. The functional weakness of the extended family which stems in large part from the separation of economic and kinship structures is thus reflected in (a) mobility *from* conjugal family (e.g., divorce rates), (b) mobility *via* conjugal family (e.g., intergroup marriage), and (c) a weakening of the familistic values per se (e.g., the value of children). Such changes have affected the range of choice in family size and freed many women for occupations outside the home.

This is complemented by the growth of the service and clerical occupations, which have been disproportionately filled with female workers. Thus the women who do go to work outside the household tend to go into the occupations specifically associated with urbanization. This is reflected in changes in the style of life of women, and of conjugal families.

It is here that the variations in family types, identified by Burgess and Locke (1945), are significant. If we consider such variations to be a function of the vast redistribution of functions which accompanies increase in scale, the basis for variation in family patterns becomes clear. Furthermore, such discussions as those of Bossard (1952) and Green (1946) suggest that variations in family pattern are indicators of variation in *style of life* and, probably, in certain aspects of social character. Such variations both reflect the variables discussed above and perpetuate and structure them in time.

Changes in the composition of population.—The third major trend refers to changes in the composition of population. *As societies increase in scale, mobility increases.* We distinguish three different concomitants of increased mobility: (1) *redistribution of population in space*, (2) *alteration in the age and sex distribution, or changes in the proportion of supporting and dependent populations,* and (3) *an increasing diversity*, with a resulting *isolation of subgroups* which are functionally significant for the total society.

1. Movements of populations which result in territorial redistribution, *the first aspect of increased mobility*, occur within a complex web of relationships involving people, objects, and ideas. Territorial redistribution is understandable only as intimately related to functional redistribution; i.e., redistribution of the population among occupations.

It is probable that such redistribution is a continual aspect of societies large in scale—studies of internal migration in the United States continue to show large interregional movements, apart from trends of population growth. The work of Thornthwaite (1934) and others indicates that since 1890 there has been a persistent *increase* in the rate of internal migration in this country. Such an increase reflects the fact that during each succeeding decade an increasingly larger proportion of urban-industrial workers has become involved in interregional movements. Such increase is associated with increasing scale, since it is associated with increasing sensitivity to economic change in the total system; thus, there are important migration differentials among occupational groups at different levels of skill, education, and income. Internal migration is no longer, then, a matter of gross movement from farm to city. It has become a system of currents: from urban to rural—not necessarily farm; from one farming region to another; from city to city; from regions of high natural increase to regions of low increase; from areas of declining industry to those of expanding opportunities.

Empirical materials on this aspect of the trend are found in the extensive literature on migration and migration differentials; Goodrich (1936), Thornthwaite (1934), and others have documented various phases of the subject for the United States. An analysis and annotation of the literature on migration differentials by Thomas (1938) is now being brought up to date by a committee of the Social Science Research Council.

2. The second aspect of increased mobility is embodied in alterations in age and sex distributions. In all large human populations there is a marked stability in the proportion of the total population in the working ages (15 to 49 or 20 to 65). The greatest variation in intergroup comparisons is found in the proportions of the population above and below these ages. Variations in the proportions of the young, the mature, and the old find their reflection in the reproductive capacity and the work capacity of the populations as a whole. This relationship can be expressed as the balance between workers and consumers or the proportion of supporting and dependent populations.

First to call attention to the significance of these broad regularities in age structure was the Swedish statistician, Sundbärg (1900). Following his lead, Pearl (1940) published statistics on the distribution of populations in a number of countries according to the threefold division of the human life cycle. Vance (1946) applied this type of analysis to the population of the United States, and drew inferences from it concerning the human resources of the South. Shevky and Williams (1949) presented data on the relation of the age structure and the sex ratio to the regularities in certain other characteristics of subpopulations in the Los Angeles Area.

From these statistics it is clear that increasing urbanization is reflected in a slow increase in the proportion of persons in the productive ages (15 to 49), due chiefly to migration—but in a striking shift in the character of the dependent population from children to the aged. Such variations reflect the selective migration by age, which is a concomitant of increase in scale. Such changes are also reflected in variation in the sex ratio. The nature of occupations which select women, for example, is such that they tend to be concentrated in urban centers; a sex variation between various parts of the society results.

3. The third aspect of increased mobility is the isolation of groups. In a society resulting from the aggregation of individuals of diverse origins and interests, there is an isolation of individuals of similar origin and position. Urban society is a heterogeneous aggregation; it is the result of change in the definition of the society to include ethnic "outside" groups, and of migration.

In urban society isolation of groups is chiefly a direct consequence of migration. The influence of friend and kin, and of the locality group, played an important part in the migration of the foreign-born. Colonies of immigrants were very frequently organized on the basis of the locality of origin. Although the characteristic development of ethnic *communities* in American cities and elsewhere is due to the convergence of a more complex set of circumstances, it is nevertheless useful to keep in mind this simpler account of the conditions of isolation. Also, empirical evidence suggests that the movement of factory workers continues to occur in neighborhood clusters, and that the influence of kin and neighbor on the direction of internal migration, and on mobility in general, is far greater than is generally assumed.

We postulate that movement of population, particularly movement in space, takes place in aggregates of varying size, persistent in form over determinable periods.[8]

The years 1840–80 were the opening period of an epoch characterized by the growing importance of cities. Throughout this period there was a steady abandonment of farm lands in the older sections of the United States and a basic reorganization of economic life in terms of the cities and the Western lands.

At the same time, the extensive application of machinery to agriculture and the opening of virgin lands (not only in North America but also in Australia and the Argentine—the "frontiers") rendered unnecessary and unprofitable much of the agricultural labor in Germany, France, and England. These changes in European agriculture were aspects of the profound reorganization of European society which was in the background of migration to America. People were continually displaced from European agriculture, and each wave of migration coincided with an era of unusual business activity and industrial expansion in the United States.

Throughout recent history the ebb and flow of immigration and the changing pattern of internal migration have moved in relation to each other. The region of origin of European migration has shifted; in different regions and countries of origin, different segments of the population were affected by this migration. There have been equally important shifts in the region of origin of migrants within the United States itself over the years.

When the foreign-born population of the United States was first enumerated in the census of 1850, 90 percent of the foreign-born were from northwestern Europe: Britain, Germany, the Scandinavian countries, the Low Countries, France, and Switzerland. Fewer than 1 percent came from southern or eastern Europe. By 1940 the proportion from northwestern Europe had fallen to about 35 percent, and the proportion from southern and eastern Europe had increased to 40 percent of the foreign-born population. In the course of this migration, between 1815 and 1914, thirty-five million Europeans were added to the American population. Those who came earlier, and came from northwestern Europe, however, attained a very different position from those who came in the "new migration."

Lloyd Warner and Leo Srole (1945) have shown an ethnic stratification in "Yankee City," in which the position of the ethnic group in *time order of migra-*

[8] On the persistence of kinship and locality ties in migration, we have particular reference to Park (1921), and to Thomas and Znaniecki (1920), as the best-known sources. On ethnic communities we refer to the summary by Ware (1937) for its brevity and excellence. The influence of kin and neighbor on the direction of movement of factory workers has been documented by Myers and MacLaurin (1943); observations on the part played by similar influences in a different setting are to be found in Goldschmidt (1947).

tion is reflected in the class position and social privilege of that group today. Old Americans are typically first in the order, followed by those northwestern Europeans and their descendants who appeared later, followed by the populations from southern and eastern Europe. (The Negroes are a special case, the heritage of domestic slavery and a number of other factors being reflected in their position.) Such an ethnic rank-order seems general in America: related to time and origin of migration, it is reflected in variations in culture, life chances, and access to economic position, status, and power.[9]

THE CONSTRUCTS AND THE INDEXES

Social rank.—The construct of social rank is specified from the changing distribution of skills in the development of modern society as a significant differentiating factor among individuals and subpopulations in modern society at one point in time. Individuals and groups are seen at this point in time as being significantly differentiated with respect to one of the long-term trends which has been important in the development of the character of modern society.

An index of social rank can be constructed from a grouping of the available census variables which are evident elements of the changing distribution of skills. We select measures of occupation, education, and rent to compose an index of social rank from among the possible measures because of their greater central importance in the changes in distribution of skills. Occupation, of course, is the key variable.

Urbanization.—In like manner a second factor, urbanization, is constructed which also is hypothesized to be a basic differentiating dimension for individuals and groups in modern society at a given point in time. This current differentiating factor is derived from the changing structure of productive activity, the second major trend in the development of modern society. Two components of this major trend are measured by an index of urbanization composed of a measure of fertility, which reflects changes in the relation of the population to the economy and changes in the function and structure of the family, and measures of house type and women in the labor force, which reflect changes in the function and structure of the family.

The third component of the changing structure of productive activity, change in the ranges of relations centered in cities, an extremely important facet of the idea of urbanization, is only indirectly measured with our index of urbanization. We hypothesize a relation between the variable, women in the labor force, and the range of relations centered in the city, but the development of an adequate index will largely depend on the possibility of the construction of a regional typology for the United States as a whole. That is, the range of relations centered in cities cannot be measured on the basis of one metropolitan area, or a selected sample of cities for which we happen to have small area statistics.

Segregation.—Finally, another construct, segregation, is derived which is hypothesized to be a third basic factor significantly differentiating modern soci-

[9] The specification of ethnic groups to be included in our index of segregation finds its rationale in an important discussion by W. Lloyd Warner and Leo Srole (1945, Chapter X).

ety. Again a dimension for the analysis of the differentiation of modern society at a given point in time is selected because it reflects in structural terms a major trend which has significantly determined the present character of that society. This trend is composed of changes in the composition of the population which are manifested by redistribution of the population in space, alteration in the age and sex composition, and the isolation of groups.[10]

Variables composing the index of segregation measure differences in individuals and groups which reflect this trend. For a subpopulation the relative concentration of specified ethnic groups, i.e., members of the "new" migration and nonwhites, is the index of segregation. The variables of foreign-born from certain countries available in the census bulletins are selected to approximate a measure of the members of the "new" migration.[11]

Urban typology.—From our analysis of social trends we identify three constructs—social rank, urbanization, and segregation—which we hypothesize are basic factors of urban differentiation and stratification. Census tract populations are grouped into types on the basis of similar configurations of scores on the indexes of the three factors. Employing the concept of attribute space, a three-dimensional space is constructed with the indexes of social rank, urbanization, and segregation as the three axes. Tracts near to one another in this social attribute space have similar patterns of scores on the three indexes and are grouped into a type. Thus, the typological analysis, which is described in detail in Chapter V, is a logically demonstrable reflection of those major changes which have produced modern, urban society.

Verification.—Two hypotheses implicit in the formulation of this social area typology have been tested for the Los Angeles Area and the San Francisco Bay Region as of 1940. The first hypothesis is that the three basic elements in the typology—social rank, urbanization, and segregation—are three factors necessary to account for the observed social differentiation between urban subpopulations; and the second hypothesis is that the indexes constructed to measure the three factors are unidimensional measuring instruments. Both of these hypotheses were tested by Bell (1952) with the use of factor analysis. The results of the factor analysis in each of the urban areas supported the hypotheses, and it was concluded that the findings represented a partial validation of the entire method of typological analysis.

---

[10] The changes in age and sex structure are aspects of increased mobility, and as such become reflected in the composition of ethnic groups. Their implications for social organization also become manifest in the economic and family structures. Since changes in age and sex structure are involved significantly in all three major trends, age and sex composition per se does not enter into the construction of any of the three indexes. (The fertility measure in the index of urbanization, however, is derived from *elements* of the age and sex variables.)

[11] Foreign-born statistics only approximate a measure of persons of the "new" migration since they measure members of the second generation to an unknown and varying degree. Also, it should be pointed out that the index of segregation as here defined is largely restricted to the United States. Different cultural contexts contain different definitions of "ethnic" groups, and these must be taken into account. Our indexes of social rank and urbanization, however, have more general application.

From the factorial analyses described above it was possible to conclude only that the three factors are *necessary* to account for the observed social variation between census tract populations. There is some evidence, however, to conclude that these factors are *adequate* as well as necessary to account for most of the observed variation between tract populations which can be extracted from the population and housing data given in the census tract bulletins. Working independently, Professor Robert C. Tryon, University of California, Berkeley, has located in the Bay Region as of 1940 three principal clusters which are comparable to social rank, urbanization, and segregation. These three clusters almost completely account for the variation between tract populations with respect to census variables. Thus, a description of the tract populations based on social rank, urbanization, and segregation captures most of the significant variation between tract populations which is revealed by census categories.

III. POSSIBLE USES OF THIS METHOD OF ANALYSIS

The underlying theory and the conceptual framework presented in Chapter II have much broader application than is indicated by the one empirical example presented in this report. To emphasize this we will attempt to indicate here some of the possible uses of this approach to social phenomena.

Various units of analysis.—To date all of the published work utilizing this method has dealt with the census tract as the unit of analysis. In both *The Social Areas of Los Angeles* (1949) and the study of the Bay Region presented in Chapter V the census tract is the unit of analysis, and the major focus of interest is the internal differentiation of a particular urban area. There is no reason, however, why a typology based on the three social dimensions—social rank, urbanization, and segregation—could not be utilized, with different specific measures in the indexes if necessary, for the study of cities with the city as the unit of analysis, for the study of regions, or even for the study of countries. The construction of a regional typology, perhaps based on the county as the unit of analysis, could represent one of the next steps in the development of the typology and a logical extension of the recent work of Hagood (1943), Bogue (1951), and others. Also, certain other populations for which information is desired might be selected as a unit of analysis. Most of the possible uses of the typology which are briefly stated in the remainder of this chapter can be accomplished at any of these levels of analysis.

The delineation of subareas.—At the various levels of analysis the typology can be used to define systematically and rigorously subareas having similar configurations of scores on the three social dimensions. Using the census tract as the unit of analysis, for example, the city can be subdivided into the mosaic of social worlds about which Wirth (1938) writes. Our term "social area" reveals the manner in which we group one set of units into larger units on the basis of their similarity with respect to their social characteristics. The concepts of "natural area" and "subculture" are not unrelated to our concept "social area" for we view a social area as containing persons with similar social positions in the larger society. The social area, however, is not bounded by the geographical frame of reference as is the natural area, nor by implications concerning the degree of interaction between persons in the local community as is the subculture. We do claim, however, that the social area generally contains persons having the same level of living, the same way of life, and the same ethnic background; and we hypothesize that persons living in a particular type of social area would systematically differ with respect to characteristic attitudes and behaviors from persons living in another type of social area.

The mere delineation of these subareas for a city, and the precision with which it is accomplished by this method, should be of descriptive value to the social scientist and city planner alike. The method presented here offers a more parsimonious and more general description of the subareas of the city than do the "community fact books."

Comparative studies at one point in time.—This method might be used to compare the social differentiation of one country with another, one region with another, or one city with another. For example, there are 12,633 census tracts in the sixty-nine urban areas tracted in 1950. As formulated here, this method allows the description of the internal social differentiation of each of the sixty-nine urban areas in a comparative framework. The census tracts falling in a particular social area are similar with respect to social rank, urbanization, and segregation whether the tracts are in Los Angeles, San Francisco, Detroit, Duluth, Rochester, or any of the other tracted urban areas. It is hypothesized, however, that the pattern of internal social differentiation—that is, the way the tracts are distributed with respect to social rank, urbanization, and segregation —would vary from one city to another, but that certain types or particular recurrent space-time-value patterns could be determined. Some of the many questions which might be answered by such a comparative study are: Do Negroes in Western cities live in the same, higher, or lower social rank areas than Negroes in cities in the South, or the Northeast, or the Midwest? Is the difference between high social rank areas and low social rank areas greater in Southern cities or in cities in the West, Northeast, Midwest, etc.? Are subareas of high urbanization (low family status) in Northeastern cities more typically of low social rank or high social rank when compared with cities in other regions? Are there areas within Western cities which have unique configurations with respect to social rank, urbanization, and segregation, or do cities in all regions have all of the possible social area types even though they may have more or fewer of a particular type? More generally, we are led to ask to what extent the observed orderly character of intra-urban forms in the metropolitan areas of the West Coast are universal properties not only of large American cities, but cities in general of the Western world and of contemporary urban life everywhere.

Similar types of questions can be raised concerning the social area distributions of census tract populations in cities of different sizes—large cities compared to medium-sized cities, and compared to smaller cities. Also, characteristic patterns of internal social differentiation can be determined for cities which have different dominant functions. The recreational city can be compared to the commercial city, or the industrial city, or the mixed city.[1] What different types of social differentiation can be located within cities performing different functions? The questions are endless, but it is our task here merely to indicate the type of problem which might be approached by the application of this typology in a comparative framework.

Similar questions can be raised at other levels of analysis. The application of the typology to the 3,103 counties for which 1950 census data are available, for example, offers an even more comprehensive and complete comparison of regional differences in social differentiation.

Comparative studies at two points in time.—As a parsimonious method for the description of changes in the social differentiation of a city, or a region, or a country, the typology can be used to test hypotheses concerning the conditions of change. The application of the typology to the 1940 and 1950 census data for the San Francisco Bay Region presented in this report represents the beginning step in such a sociological study. Our purpose in this report is to illustrate the application of the procedures in a comparative framework and to demonstrate just exactly what type of information the typology alone yields. The next and more important question, however, is what has brought about these observed

---

[1] See Harris (1943) for a functional classification of cities in the United States.

changes in the social differentiation of the Bay Region? To answer this question we must examine data other than those given in the census tract statistics. We must look to data external to our typology, e.g., movements of industry and commerce, shifts in the location of governmental agencies, as well as changes in the *national* economy, migration trends, and the like.

In this type of study the changes in the social differentiation of a population described by the application of the typology are considered to be dependent variables and the conditions for change are searched out and systematically related to the broader social structural changes.

A framework for the execution of other types of research.—While correlations based upon census tract averages must be used with caution,[2] the typological analysis for a particular city offers an efficient method for studying the attitudes and behaviors of individuals living in the various types of neighborhoods in the city. Again the geographical distribution of a particular attitude or behavior would not be of primary interest. Rather, the relationship between the attitude or behavior and type of community as to social rank, urbanization, and segregation would be of primary importance. For example, Aubrey Wendling (1954) has related suicide rates in San Francisco census tracts to the social rank, urbanization, and segregation scores of the tracts. A considerable amount of the variation in suicide rates can be explained by these three factors. Other variables which might be studied for which data are readily available are number of registered voters, people's choices of candidates as measured by voting behavior, mental disorders, crime rates, etc. In each case the particular behavior would be related to the social character of the tract population as measured by the three factors: social rank, urbanization, and segregation.

In addition to its use as a frame for the manipulation of available statistics such as crime rates, suicide rates, and others, the typology can be used as a frame for the design and execution of field studies. It is our belief that detailed field investigations of subareas within the city can profit from this typological analysis in at least two ways. First, the typological analysis will aid in the location of the kind of subarea which is to be studied. The problem to be investigated may require that a particular type of subarea be singled out for study. A census tract's scores on social rank, urbanization, and segregation define important aspects of the social character of the tract population. In this operation the social area analysis is used as a sampling device during the design of the study. Second, the typological analysis provides a generality to field investigations of urban subareas often lacking in discrete studies of some specific aspect of urban life. This typology offers to such intensive studies articulation and integration with a larger mass of ordered data. Two studies now nearing completion, one in Los Angeles and one in San Francisco, were designed, in part, to test the utility of this typology as a frame for the execution of intensive studies of urban subareas.

While this brief statement by no means exhausts the possible uses to which this method of analysis might be put, it does suggest that the empirical example which follows in Chapter V is only one of many which might have been selected for presentation.

[2] On this point see Robinson (1950).

IV. REVISIONS

The minor modifications in the typology proposed in this chapter will allow the application of the typology to the 1940 and 1950 census data for all tracted American cities in a comparative framework. Also these modifications will increase the analytic power of the typology as a method for the comparative study of urban internal differentiation. However, a word of caution is in order here. We do not propose that the typology as here constructed is free from flaws. Many unresolved questions remain in our own minds. For example, is there a better common base for the standardization of the index scores than the ranges in Los Angeles as of 1940? Is it possible to establish some zero point for each of the indexes so that an analysis of changes in index scores would be more meaningful? Should more variables be used to measure each of the indexes? If so, what variables are most valid and reliable for use in all cities? Should an absolute cutting point in the index of segregation be established instead of allowing the cutting point to remain relative to the proportions of subordinate ethnic groups in a particular urban area? Satisfactory solutions to these and other questions will increase the reliability and validity of the typology. Solutions to these questions, however, largely depend upon experimentation and the testing of various alternatives for many cities at once, which was beyond the scope of our resources. The procedures as herein specified, however, allow the method to be used now as a framework for the comparative study of the internal social differentiation of urban areas. It is our hope that our colleagues will test, apply, and criticize them, and that, as a result, further revisions can be made which will improve the typology as an instrument for the comparative study of cities.

The index of social rank.—One of the three basic social dimensions used in the Shevky-Williams typology is social rank. The index of social rank, as originally constructed by Shevky and Williams, was based upon measures of occupation, education, and rent. While these variables appear to be adequate measures of social rank for census tract populations in 1940, several difficulties arise concerning the use of the rent measure in 1950. The rent measure used by Shevky and Williams in 1940 was based on "contract or estimated monthly rent." Estimated monthly rent, however, was not used as a census category in 1950, so the only rent figures for 1940 and 1950 which can be compared are based on "contract monthly rent." One of the reasons that this measure is unsatisfactory is that the percentage of dwellings which are rented varies greatly by census tract. Thus, in some tracts the median contract monthly rent may be based on only a very few of the dwellings in the census tract, and these may be quite atypical of the rest of the dwellings in the tract.

Also, the rent controls introduced by the federal government during World War II, especially during 1942 and 1943, seriously affect the validity of a rent measure being used as an index of social rank. Rent controls were still effective in some form in most cities when the census was taken in 1950. For example, from 1940 to 1950 disposable income and consumer expenditures in the United States increased about 170 percent, compared with an average rent increase of 25 percent (Grebler, 1952). This discrepancy between income increases and rent increases seems to reduce the utility of a measure of rent as an index of social rank.

There is an additional difficulty in using rent as a measure of the social rank of census tract populations. This too is a consequence of rent controls. Rent controls were differentially applied to certain segments of the population. For instance, some sections of a city may have been composed mostly of renter-occupied dwellings to which rent controls applied; other sections may have been composed mostly of new or converted units to which rent controls did not apply and for which rents were generally higher than for comparable units under rent controls (Grebler, 1952). A comparison of average rents for a given census tract in 1940 and 1950 may show little difference, reflecting the fact that most of the rental units were controlled in the tract; or such a comparison may reveal a large increase in average rent, reflecting the fact that the tract consists mostly of new or converted rental units not covered by rent controls. Consequently, a measure based on rent is inadequate as an index of social rank, both when comparing different census tracts in 1950 and when comparing the same census tracts in 1940 and 1950.

The possibility of substituting some measure of income for the rent measure in the index of social rank was explored, but there are at least two difficulties with the use of an income measure. First, no income data by census tracts for 1940 comparable to the 1950 income data are available, thus making 1940 and 1950 income comparisons by census tracts impossible. Second, the income data reported by census tracts for 1950 have defects as an index of social rank when comparing median incomes for different tracts in 1950. The income figures presented in the census represent the amount of income received by family units and unrelated individuals. Since the proportion of unrelated individuals varies markedly from tract to tract, the median income for a tract reflects a built-in bias tending to decrease the "social rank" of a tract which contains a large proportion of unrelated individuals.

As a result of these considerations, the index of social rank was modified to contain just two measures, namely, occupation and education. It is suggested that the revised index of social rank, containing just the two measures, be used for the analysis of census data for 1940 and 1950, thus allowing the direct comparison of index scores. This revision, and the others to be specified, have been incorporated in the empirical case presented in Chapter V.

Consistent with Bell's proposal (1953) the occupation and education ratios are standardized to a 0 to 100 range based on the actual ranges of those variables in Los Angeles in 1940. Thus, a single scale is established to measure the social rank of census tract populations in different cities and at different times.

The index of urbanization.—No changes are necessary in the index of urbanization for the comparison of 1940 and 1950 tracted cities. The three measures used are fertility, women in the labor force, and single-family dwelling units. Comparable statistics are available for all three measures by census tracts for cities tracted in 1940 and 1950. The index of urbanization is standardized to the ranges of its variables in Los Angeles in 1940. Thus scores on the index of urbanization also are comparable from one city to another and one decade to another.[1]

The index of segregation.—The third basic dimension used to determine the

---

[1] See Appendix B.

social position of a census tract population is segregation. A modification in the index of segregation consistent with the revisions in the index of isolation and the group segregation ratio suggested by Bell (1954) seems desirable.[2] The standardization of the groups composing the index of segregation to include those groups which traditionally have held subordinate status in American society is recommended. Thus, the segregation status of a census tract population would be determined by the percent of the tract population represented by certain subordinate groups. Following the categories used by the U.S. Census Bureau in 1950[3] in the bulletins for tracted cities, these groups are Negro; Other Races; and foreign-born white from Poland, Czechoslovakia, Hungary, Yugoslavia, U.S.S.R., Lithuania, Finland, Rumania, Greece, Italy, Other Europe, Asia, French Canada, Mexico, and Other America.[4]

In the prior applications of the typology by Shevky and Williams (1949) in Los Angeles and by Bell (1953) in the San Francisco Bay Region, groups were selected for inclusion in the computation of the index of segregation depending on the extent of the group's residential concentration in the city as a whole as measured by the index of isolation. The difficulty with this procedure is not only that the final composite measure of a census tract's ethnic status (index of segregation) is likely to vary from one city to another, thus reducing the possibility of direct comparisons,[5] but also that groups may be highly concentrated in some residential areas and absent from others and be superordinate groups rather than subordinate groups. For instance, in a city containing only whites and nonwhites, in which the nonwhites are completely segregated, the whites are necessarily completely segregated also. Thus, selecting the groups which are segregated in a city to measure the ethnic status (index of segregation) of each census tract does not necessarily include only those groups having subordinate status. Including the ethnic groups listed above in the measure of ethnic status of a census tract population, however, allows the direct comparison of index of segregation scores from one city to another and seems to be a generally meaningful statistic for American cities.[6]

The division of social space.—Shevky and Williams construct types of census tract populations which they call social areas, by grouping together those census tracts having similar configurations of scores on the indexes of social rank,

---

[2] The index of segregation (or index of ethnic status) measures *the degree of segregation of a census tract*; i.e., it measures the presence or absence of certain racial, nationality, and cultural groups in a census tract. The index of isolation and the group segregation ratio (pp. 44–48) measure *the degree of segregation of groups* over the city as a whole.

[3] Comparable groups for 1940 census categories are given in the section on computational procedures.

[4] See Chapter VI for additional comments on these groups.

[5] Using the procedure of including in the index of segregation only those groups with indexes of isolation in excess of 3.00, Shevky and Williams selected Negroes, Orientals, Mexicans, Italians, and Russians to compose the index of segregation in Los Angeles in 1940; Bell, however, using the same procedure, included only Negroes, Orientals, Mexicans, and Italians in his study of the San Francisco Bay Region in 1940.

[6] For a discussion of the status of American ethnic groups, see Warner and Srole (1945). Also see Shevky and Williams (1949: 19).

urbanization, and segregation. First, they construct a two-dimensional attribute space with the index of social rank as the base and the index of urbanization as the vertical axis. Second, they divide the social space into nine cells by dividing the base, social rank, into three intervals of approximate thirds of the range, indicating low, middle, and high social rank; and by dividing the vertical axis, urbanization, into three intervals with the middle or average interval determined by the space of two standard errors about the regression line of urbanization related to social rank. By plotting the census tracts in the social space according to their scores on the indexes of social rank and urbanization the position of the tracts in the nine cells can be determined. Census tracts located in the same cell were considered to be of the same social area type. Figure IV-1 shows the division of the social space as originally constructed by Shevky and Williams.

The index of segregation is included in the typology by distinguishing be-

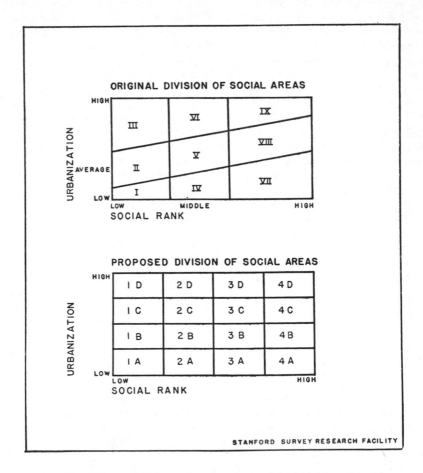

FIG. IV-1.—Social area keys based on original division of social areas and proposed division of social areas.

tween census tracts with high indexes of segregation and census tracts with low indexes of segregation, making a total of eighteen possible social area types.

The revision suggested here concerns the division of social space. As can be seen in Figure IV-1, the proposed division of social space has sixteen instead of nine cells. It is proposed that the base, social rank, be divided into four intervals, social rank scores of 0 to 24, 25 to 49, 50 to 74, and 75 to 100, each comprising a separate interval on the social rank scale; and that the vertical axis, urbanization, be divided into four intervals, urbanization scores of 0 to 24, 25 to 49, 50 to 74, and 75 to 100, each comprising a separate interval on the urbanization scale.

Two considerations favor this proposal. The first is that the social areas are made more homogeneous with respect to social rank and urbanization by more narrowly defining the limits of the social areas. This is particularly important in view of the standardization of social rank and urbanization scores to the ranges of those variables in Los Angeles as of 1940. The more refined cuts in the social space serve to maintain the differentiating power of the typology in making an intracity analysis even when a city has ranges on the indexes of social rank and urbanization smaller than those ranges in Los Angeles. If the broader divisions of the social areas were used, some of the smaller tracted cities would be completely contained in only a few social areas.

The second consideration concerns the use of the regression line of urbanization on social rank in making the divisions in the continuum of urbanization. The original division of the continuum of urbanization was made by drawing two lines parallel to the regression line one standard error on either side of the regression line (see Fig. IV-1). The divisions of the urbanization continuum were originally made in this way, so that the divisions would follow the shape of the bivariate distribution of urbanization on social rank. That is, the cuts in urbanization reflected the relation between the index of social rank and the index of urbanization for Los Angeles in 1940. Since the relation of social rank and urbanization varies from one urban area to another (e.g., Los Angeles in 1940, $r = .41$; San Francisco Bay Region in 1940, $r = .25$) and from one time to another (e.g., San Francisco Bay Region in 1940, $r = .25$; San Francisco Bay Region in 1950, $r = .13$), it would seem desirable not to restrict the divisions in the urbanization continuum to the relation of urbanization and social rank in the Los Angeles Area in 1940. It is proposed here that the divisions in the index of urbanization be freed from conformity to the shape of any particular distribution of urbanization and social rank, that the divisions should be arbitrarily set at urbanization scores of 25, 50, and 75, and that the division be made parallel with the base, social rank. (see Fig. IV-1).

V. THE SOCIAL AREAS OF THE SAN FRANCISCO BAY REGION, 1940 AND 1950

The analytic utility of the Shevky-Williams typology will be illustrated here by its use in the analysis of certain aspects of the social structure of the San Francisco Bay Region in 1940 and 1950. The suggested revisions in the typology will be incorporated in the following presentation, so that its use in analyzing the 1940 and 1950 data for the Bay Region may serve as a model for the use of the typology in studying the social stratification and differentiation of other urban centers. The purpose is to demonstrate the use of the typology as a framework for the comparative study of the internal differentiation of American cities, rather than to completely exploit all available materials concerning the San Francisco Bay Region.

The basic data.—The basic data for the study are contained in the 1940 and 1950 census tract bulletins of the U.S. Census Bureau. The census tract is the unit of analysis, and there were 243 census tracts included in the study in 1940 and 244 census tracts included in 1950.[1] Certain tracts containing a total tract population too small to permit statistical analysis or containing large institutional populations are excluded from the analysis.[2]

Figure V-1 contains a map outlining the area included in the analysis. The Bay Area cities included in the analysis are San Francisco, Oakland, Berkeley, Albany, Emeryville, Piedmont, Alameda, San Leandro, Richmond, and El Cerrito. Unfortunately, data by census tracts are not available for adjacent areas which represent a functioning part of the larger San Francisco Bay Region. For example, certain areas in Marin County, south of San Francisco on the peninsula, south of San Leandro, and east of Berkeley also should be included in the analysis. However, the large majority of the total Bay Region population is contained in the area for which data are available.

Also contained in Figure V-1 is a generalized land use map showing for the region under study those areas that were vacant or predominantly industrially, commercially, residentially, or publicly occupied in 1950.[3]

Distribution of the population by social areas.—In 1940 the population of the Bay Region used in the study was 1,119,493; by 1950 the population of the same area had increased to 1,509,678, a percentage increase of 34.9 percent.

The first comparison that can be made is between the social area distributions of the populations at the two periods. The social area distribution of the census tract populations for 1940 is given in Figure V-2; the distribution for 1950 is contained in Figure V-3. Comparing the social area distribution of the census tracts in 1940 with the social area distribution of the census tracts in 1950, certain similarities can be seen. First is the relatively low correlation between social

---

[1] The census tract designated AC-19 in 1940 was divided into two tracts in 1950, AC-19 and AC-20.

[2] The tracts excluded are F-1, Fort Miley; I-1, Golden Gate Park; K-5, Warehouse Area; R-1, Ocean Beach, west of Lake Merced, and Farallon Islands; C-1, the Presidio; and S-1, Ships at Sea—registered from San Francisco as home port (S-1 as a separate category did not exist in 1950).

[3] Original data for the generalized land use maps were obtained from maps made available by the San Francisco, Oakland, and Berkeley City Planning Commissions.

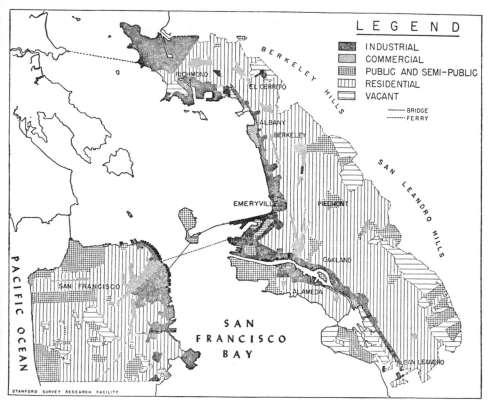

Fig. V-1.—Residential, commercial, industrial, public, and unoccupied areas in the San Francisco Bay Region, 1950.

rank and urbanization in 1940 ($r = .25$) and 1950 ($r = .13$).[4] Second, census tracts with high indexes of segregation predominated at the lower levels of social rank, while tracts with low indexes of segregation predominated at the higher levels of social rank in both 1940 and 1950. The Pearsonian correlation between social rank and segregation in 1940 was $-.40$; it increased to $-.50$ in 1950. That is, census tracts characterized by high social rank scores tended to contain few members of the combined subordinate ethnic groups.

Another similarity in the distribution of census tracts in 1940 and 1950 can be noted from Figures V-2 and V-3. There was a general tendency for segregated tracts to occur at the higher levels of urbanization. Although the over-all correlation between urbanization and segregation in 1940 ($r = .17$) and in 1950 ($r = .16$) was only slight, the relation was more marked at the higher levels of social rank at both times. For higher levels of social rank, there was a definite

---

[4] It is significant that the correlation between social rank and urbanization was lower in 1950 than in 1940. This would indicate that it is even more important to keep these two factors logically discrete in 1950 than in 1940.

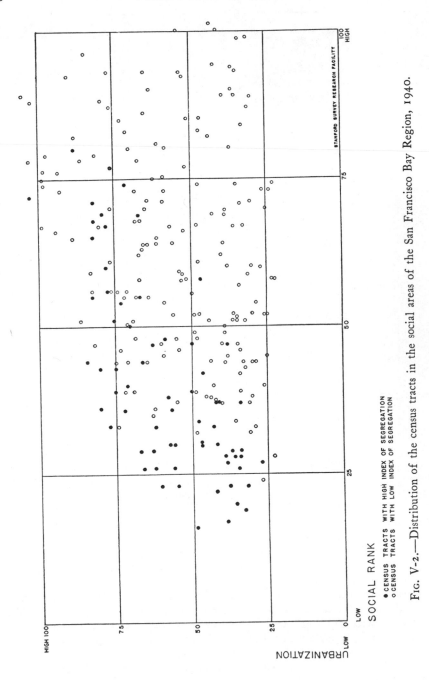

FIG. V-2.—Distribution of the census tracts in the social areas of the San Francisco Bay Region, 1940.

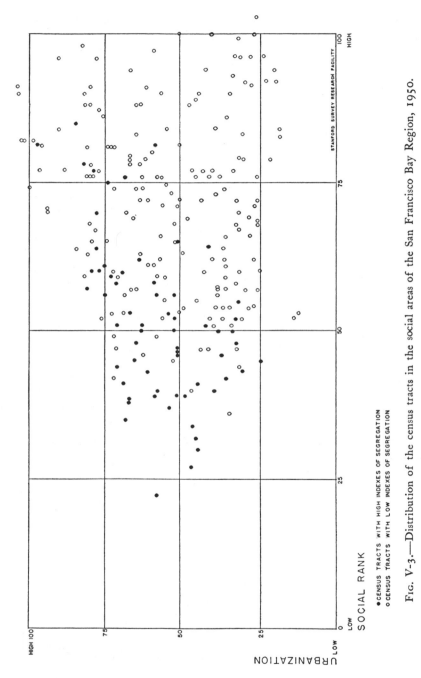

Fig. V-3.—Distribution of the census tracts in the social areas of the San Francisco Bay Region, 1950.

tendency for the segregated tracts to occur at higher levels of urbanization (i.e., to occur in areas characterized by lower family status).

Figures V-4 and V-5, which contain the number and percent of persons by social areas for 1940 and 1950 respectively, also show these similarities. How-

TOTAL POPULATION

	35,915	116,614	73,275
10,718	169,594	197,579	57,170
41,237	190,177	153,979	64,537
	1,852	6,846	

POPULATION

	3.2	10.4	6.5
1.0	15.1	17.6	5.1
3.7	17.0	13.8	5.8
	.2	.6	

PER CENT POPULATION

LOW INDEX OF SEGREGATION

	8,965	58,848	64,647
0	74,200	171,485	57,170
4,136	127,565	151,059	64,537
	1,852	6,846	

	.8	5.2	5.8
0	6.6	15.3	5.1
.4	11.4	13.5	5.8
	.2	.6	

HIGH INDEX OF SEGREGATION

	26,950	57,766	8,628
10,718	95,394	26,094	0
37,101	62,612	2,920	0
	0	0	

POPULATION

	2.4	5.2	.7
1.0	8.5	2.3	0
3.3	5.6	.3	0
	0	0	

PER CENT POPULATION

URBANIZATION (HIGH → LOW)

1 D	2 D	3 D	4 D
1 C	2 C	3 C	4 C
1 B	2 B	3 B	4 B
1 A	2 A	3 A	4 A

LOW   HIGH
SOCIAL RANK

STANFORD SURVEY RESEARCH FACILITY

FIG. V-4.—Number and percent of the population of the San Francisco Bay Region in each social area, 1940.

ever, there are certain differences in the social area distributions of 1940 and 1950 as well as similarities. The most marked change results from the general increase in social rank from 1940 to 1950. In 1940 4.7 percent of the total Bay Region population lived in the lowest social rank social areas, in 1950 only 0.1 percent of the total population was located in these lowest social rank social areas. The next lowest social rank group of social areas 2A, 2B, 2C, and 2D contained 35.5 percent of the population in 1940, but contained only 23.7 percent of the population in 1950. On the other hand, the highest social rank areas 4A, 4B, 4C, and 4D contained 32.0 percent of the population in 1950, but contained only 17.4 percent of the population in 1940. Thus, there was a general shift of census tract populations into social areas of higher social rank from 1940 to 1950.

Another change can be seen by comparing the 1940 and 1950 social area distributions. Although much less marked than the increase in social rank, there is a decided decrease in urbanization (increase in family status) from 1940 to 1950. This increase in family status is especially marked in the higher social rank social areas. For example, the highest urbanization social areas 1D, 2D, 3D, and 4D contained 20.1 percent of the population in 1940; by 1950, however, the percent of the population contained in these social areas had decreased to 16.0 percent. Also, the lowest urbanization social areas 1A, 2A, 3A, and 4A increased from 0.8 percent of the population in 1940 to 2.5 percent in 1950. In addition, the next lowest urbanization social areas 1B, 2B, 3B, and 4B increased from 40.3 percent in 1940 to 47.6 percent in 1950.

The investigator interested in a further analysis of the changes in social rank and urbanization would construct a figure giving the median values of the index components for 1940 and 1950. Such a figure is presented in Figure V-6. These ratios were obtained by grouping the census tracts by 1940 social areas, then computing the medians of the index components for each social area for 1940 and 1950. Thus, each median given in Figure V-6 for 1940 and 1950 refers to the same group of tracts ordered with respect to 1940 social areas. For example, in the tracts composing social area 2A in 1940, the median number of craftsmen, operatives, and laborers in 1940 is 696 per 1,000 employed persons; whereas, for those same tracts the median number of craftsmen, operatives, and laborers is 558 per 1,000 employed persons in 1950. This indicates that, as measured by occupation, the social rank of those tracts composing social area 2A in 1940 has increased. To facilitate an assessment of the changes in each index component from 1940 to 1950, Figure V-7 can be constructed by subtracting the 1940 medians from the 1950 medians for each set of tracts grouped by 1940 social areas. Thus, differential change in the medians by social areas can be easily noted. The general increase in social rank as measured by occupation and education can be seen by referring to Figures V-6 and V-7.[5] The median number of craftsmen, operatives, and laborers per 1,000 employed persons decreased

[5] Since a decrease in the relative number of craftsmen, operatives, and laborers and a decrease in the relative number of persons who have completed grade school only represents an increase in the social rank of a census tract population, the signs of the differences given in Figure V-7 for "operatives and laborers" and "grade school" must be reversed when thinking in terms of increases or decreases in social rank.

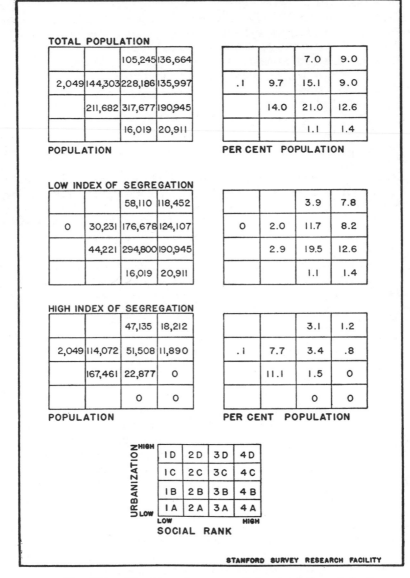

TOTAL POPULATION

		105,245	36,664
2,049	144,303	228,186	135,997
	211,682	317,677	190,945
		16,019	20,911

POPULATION

		7.0	9.0
.1	9.7	15.1	9.0
		14.0	21.0	12.6
		1.1	1.4

PER CENT POPULATION

LOW INDEX OF SEGREGATION

		58,110	118,452
0	30,231	176,678	124,107
	44,221	294,800	190,945
		16,019	20,911

		3.9	7.8
0	2.0	11.7	8.2
	2.9	19.5	12.6
		1.1	1.4

HIGH INDEX OF SEGREGATION

		47,135	18,212
2,049	114,072	51,508	11,890
	167,461	22,877	0
		0	0

POPULATION

		3.1	1.2
.1	7.7	3.4	.8
	11.1	1.5	0
		0	0

PER CENT POPULATION

URBANIZATION HIGH				
	1 D	2 D	3 D	4 D
	1 C	2 C	3 C	4 C
	1 B	2 B	3 B	4 B
LOW	1 A	2 A	3 A	4 A

LOW   HIGH

SOCIAL RANK

STANFORD SURVEY RESEARCH FACILITY

FIG. V-5.—Number and percent of the population of the San Francisco Bay Region in each social area, 1950.

from 1940 to 1950 in every 1940 social area except social areas 2D, 4D, and 4B, the largest decreases being in social areas 2A (from 696 to 558), 3A (from 382 to 290), 1B (from 653 to 585), and 2B (from 538 to 474). The greatest increases in social rank due to occupational shifts came in the low social rank, low urbanization social areas.

Turning to the social rank changes accounted for by changes in the measure of education, the same general increase in social rank can be seen. The median number of persons with education terminated who had completed only grade school decreased in every 1940 social area population from 1940 to 1950. The largest decreases in the education ratio occurred in 1940 social areas 1B (from 681 to 466), 2A (from 546 to 344), 2B (from 538 to 394), and 1C (from 740 to 609). The greatest increases in social rank due to educational shifts occurred in the low social rank social area populations.

By transforming the occupational and educational ratios given in Figure V-6 into standard scores by the formula given in Appendix B, it can be determined that increases in the index of social rank reflect changes in education more than changes in occupation.

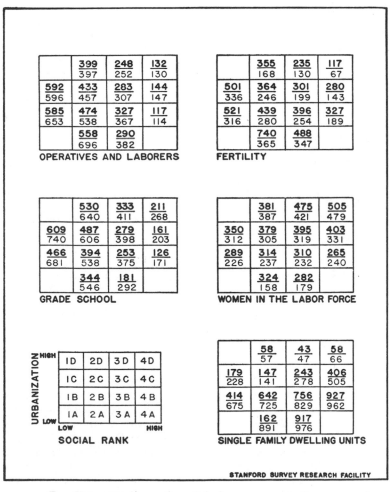

Fig. V-6.—Median ratios of index components for 1940 and 1950 for 1940 social areas.

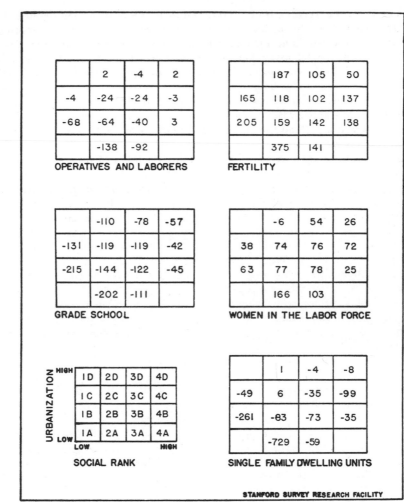

	2	-4	2
-4	-24	-24	-3
-68	-64	-40	3
	-138	-92	

OPERATIVES AND LABORERS

	187	105	50
165	118	102	137
205	159	142	138
	375	141	

FERTILITY

	-110	-78	-57
-131	-119	-119	-42
-215	-144	-122	-45
	-202	-111	

GRADE SCHOOL

	-6	54	26
38	74	76	72
63	77	78	25
	166	103	

WOMEN IN THE LABOR FORCE

HIGH				
	1D	2D	3D	4D
	1C	2C	3C	4C
	1B	2B	3B	4B
LOW	1A	2A	3A	4A

URBANIZATION (vertical axis, LOW to HIGH); horizontal axis LOW to HIGH

SOCIAL RANK

	1	-4	-8
-49	6	-35	-99
-261	-83	-73	-35
	-729	-59	

SINGLE FAMILY DWELLING UNITS

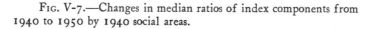

STANFORD SURVEY RESEARCH FACILITY

Fig. V-7.—Changes in median ratios of index components from 1940 to 1950 by 1940 social areas.

Similarly, one can analyze further the observed changes in urbanization. The 1940 and 1950 medians by 1940 social areas for the components of the index of urbanization also are given in Figure V-6, and the changes are given in Figure V-7. The components of the index of urbanization do not change in the same way from 1940 to 1950. Fertility generally increased, resulting in *decreased urbanization scores* (increased family status); the proportion of women in the labor force generally increased, resulting in *increased urbanization scores* (decreased family status); and the proportion of single-family dwelling units generally decreased, resulting in *increased urbanization scores* (decreased family status).

Changes in the fertility ratios from 1940 to 1950 were generally much larger than changes in the medians of either of the other two components of the index of urbanization. The median ratio of children under age five to every 1,000 women in the 15 to 44 age group increased in every 1940 social area population from 1940 to 1950.[6] The larger increases in fertility generally occurred in the lower urbanization social areas at every level of social rank, and in the lower social rank social areas at every level of urbanization. Social areas 2A (from 365 to 740), 1B (from 316 to 521), 2D (from 168 to 355), and 1C (from 336 to 501) had the largest decreases in urbanization due to changes in fertility from 1940 to 1950.

Changes in the other two measures composing the index of urbanization were not consistent generally with the changes in fertility. The median number of women in the labor force per 1,000 women of fourteen years of age and over increased in every 1940 social area population except 2D, thus generally increasing urbanization scores. Likewise, general decreases in the median number of single-family dwelling units per 1,000 dwellings contributed to increases in urbanization scores. Only social areas 2C and 2D had decreases in urbanization due to increases in the relative number of single-family dwellings.

Shifts in the fertility ratio tended to predominate in 1940 social areas of high urbanization, reducing the urbanization scores for census tracts in these social areas; while shifts in the relative number of women in the labor force combined with shifts in the relative number of single-family dwellings tended to predominate in 1940 social areas characterized by low urbanization, increasing the urbanization scores for census tracts in these social areas.[7]

A researcher who wanted to describe the nature of the social areas at a particular time would construct a figure like Figure V-8. This contains the median ratios of index components for 1950 by 1950 social areas. These ratios serve to illustrate further the configuration of demographic characteristics defining the social areas. For example, census tract populations in social area 4D, the *highest social rank and highest urbanization* social area, contained few craftsmen, operatives, and laborers (median ratio = 176); few persons having completed grade school only (median ratio = 226); low fertility ratios (median ratio = 155); many women in the labor force (median ratio = 498); and few single-family dwelling units (median ratio = 58). On the other hand, the census tract population in social area 1C, the *lowest social rank* social area, contained many craftsmen, operatives, and laborers (median ratio = 624); and many persons having completed grade school only (median ratio = 699). Census tracts in social area 3A, one of the *lowest urbanization* social areas, contained high fertility ratios (median ratio = 689); few women in the labor force (median ratio = 293); and many single-family dwellings (median ratio = 916).

Age and sex characteristics.—Changes in two other important characteristics of urban subareas may interest the research worker. Figure V-9 contains age and

[6] This trend, of course, is consistent with the general increase in birth rates and fertility ratios in recent years for the United States.

[7] Preliminary profile analysis of the intercorrelations among the index components for 1950 indicates that the three factors were as clear-cut in 1950 as they were in 1940. In addition, the factors of social rank and urbanization were more independent in 1950 than they were in 1940.

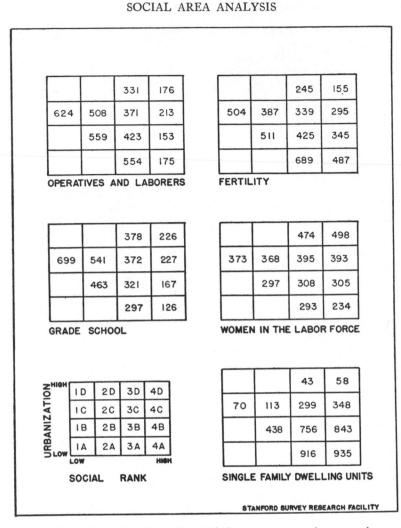

		331	176
624	508	371	213
	559	423	153
		554	175

OPERATIVES AND LABORERS

		245	155
504	387	339	295
	511	425	345
		689	487

FERTILITY

		378	226
699	541	372	227
	463	321	167
		297	126

GRADE SCHOOL

		474	498
373	368	395	393
	297	308	305
		293	234

WOMEN IN THE LABOR FORCE

URBANIZATION (HIGH → LOW)

1D	2D	3D	4D
1C	2C	3C	4C
1B	2B	3B	4B
1A	2A	3A	4A

LOW — HIGH

SOCIAL RANK

		43	58
70	113	299	348
	438	756	843
		916	935

SINGLE FAMILY DWELLING UNITS

STANFORD SURVEY RESEARCH FACILITY

Fig. V-8.—Median ratios of index components for 1950 by 1950 social areas.

sex characteristics for 1940 and 1950 by 1940 social areas, and Figure V-10 contains the changes in age and sex characteristics obtained by subtracting the 1940 values for each social area from the 1950 values. The median number of men per every 100 women decreased somewhat in every social area except the three highest social rank 1940 social areas 4B, 4C, and 4D; and the low social rank social area 1C. The largest decrease in the relative number of men occurred in social area 2D, the lower social rank and highest urbanization social area, in which the median number of men per every 100 women decreased from 322 in 1940 to 247 in 1950.

The general pattern of changes in the age distributions of the social areas was for the percent of persons in the youth group (age 0 to 14) to increase; the percent of persons in the middle group (age 15 to 49) to decrease; and the percent of persons classified as older age (age 50 and over) to increase, although the proportion of older aged persons decreased in four 1940 social areas. The percent of persons under age fifteen increased in every 1940 social area population from 1940 to 1950 except 4D in which there was no change. The largest increases were in the low urbanization social areas and the low social rank social areas. These occurred in social areas 2A (from 24 to 37 percent), 2B (from 20 to 27 percent), 1B (from 23 to 28 percent), 1C (from 20 to 25 percent), and 3B (from 19 to 24 percent).

The percent of 1940 social area populations represented by persons in the

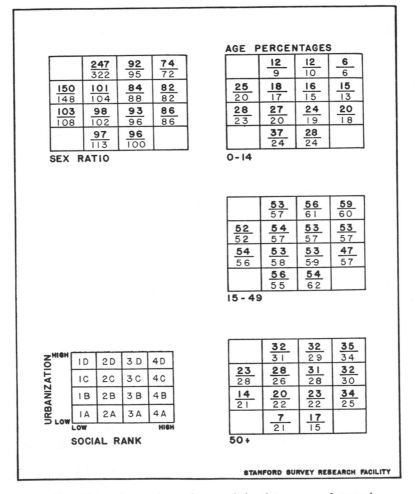

Fig. V-9.—Age and sex characteristics for 1940 and 1950 by 1940 social areas.

age group 15 to 49 decreased from 1940 to 1950 in every social area except social areas 1C and 2A. The largest decreases in the relative number of persons in this middle age group were in the high social rank and low urbanization social areas 4B (from 57 to 47 percent), 3A (from 62 to 54 percent), and 3B (from 59 to 53 percent).

While the percent of persons over age fifty increased in most of the social areas, the percent of persons over age fifty decreased in the lowest social rank social areas 1B (from 21 to 14 percent) and 1C (from 28 to 23 percent); and also decreased in the lower social rank lower urbanization social areas 2A (from 21 to 7 percent) and 2B (from 22 to 20 percent). The highest social rank

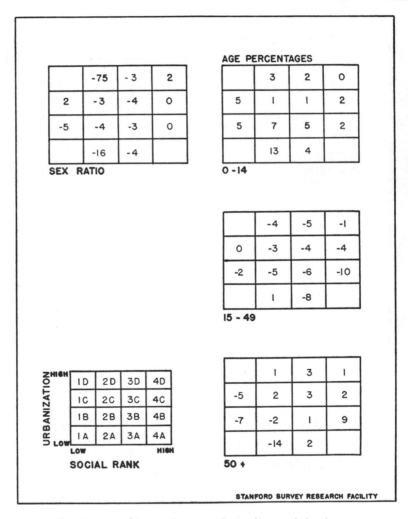

Fig. V-10.—Changes in age and sex characteristics from 1940 to 1950 by 1940 social areas.

lower urbanization social area 4B had the largest increase (from 25 to 34 percent) in the proportion of older age persons.

To describe further the nature of the social areas an investigator would construct a figure like Figure V-11, in which the age and sex characteristics for 1950 by 1950 social areas are given. Notice that the general variation in the sex ratio by the 1950 social areas was similar to that shown in Figure V-9 for the 1940 social areas. At the highest level of social rank the sex ratio decreased with increasing urbanization, social area 4D having the lowest number of men per 100 women both in 1940 and 1950. At the lower levels of social rank the sex ratio tended to increase with increasing urbanization. In 1950 social area 2C

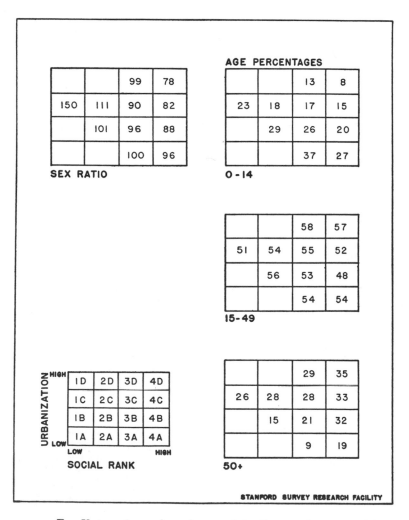

FIG. V-11.—Age and sex characteristics for 1950 by 1950 social areas.

had a sex ratio of 111 compared with a sex ratio of 101 for social area 2B; in 1940 social area 1C had a sex ratio of 148 compared with a sex ratio of 108 for social area 1B, and 2D had a sex ratio of 322 compared with a sex ratio of 113 for social area 2A.

Another similarity in the 1940 and 1950 median sex ratios by social areas is the uniform decrease in the sex ratio with increasing social rank at every level of urbanization. Without exception the number of men per every 100 women decreased as social rank increased for every level of urbanization.

		HAIGHT-ASHBURY (SF) CIVIC CENTER (SF)	PACIFIC HEIGHTS (SF) MARINA (SF) DOWNTOWN COMMERCIAL (SF) NOB HILL (SF) LAKE MERRITT (O)
	BERNAL HEIGHTS (SF) FRUITVALE (O) EMERYVILLE	RICHMOND (SF) PRESIDIO TERRACE (SF) BUENA VISTA (SF) EUREKA VALLEY (SF) TEMESCAL (O) EAST LAKE (O)	PARNASSUS HEIGHTS (SF) MOUNT SUTRO (SF) ELMWOOD (B) GRAND AVENUE (O)
	VISITACION VALLEY (SF) ELMHURST (O) MELROSE (O)	BAYSHORE (SF) PORTOLA (SF) LAUREL (O) DIAMOND (O) ALLENDALE (O) ALBANY SAN LEANDRO EL CERRITO	INGLESIDE TERRACE (SF) ST. FRANCIS WOOD (SF) SEACLIFF (SF) BALBOA TERRACE (SF) CLAREMONT (O,B) TRESTLE GLEN (O) NORTH BERKELEY (B) PIEDMONT
		BROOKFIELD (O)	MONTCLAIR (O) OAK KNOLL (O) SHEFFIELD (O)

(SF) SAN FRANCISCO   (O) OAKLAND   (B) BERKELEY

LOW INDEX OF SEGREGATION

Fig. V-12.—Selected places representative of the social areas of the San Francisco Bay Region, 1950 (low index of segregation).

The age distributions by social areas were also similar in 1940 and 1950 (see Figs. V-9 and V-11). The percent of each social area population in the youth group for both times decreased with increasing urbanization at every level of social rank. Also, while the pattern is less clear in 1940, the percent in the youth group decreased with increasing social rank at both times at every level of urbanization. The percent in the older age group increased with increasing urbanization for comparable levels of social rank, and increased with increasing social rank for every level of urbanization in 1950. Social area 4D, the highest social rank and highest urbanization social area, contained the smallest proportion of youth and the largest proportion of older age persons in 1940 and 1950.

Geographical location of social areas.—City planners, especially, may be interested in relating local community names to the social area analysis. Identifying place names characteristic of the 1950 social areas of the San Francisco Bay Region are given in Figures V-12 and V-13.[8] These place names are illustrative of the various neighborhoods in the different social areas. Places illustrative of

---

[8] Identifying place names for every census tract are contained in Appendix A. Also, census tract scores on the indexes of social rank, urbanization, and segregation along with social area designations for 1940 and 1950 are given in Appendix A.

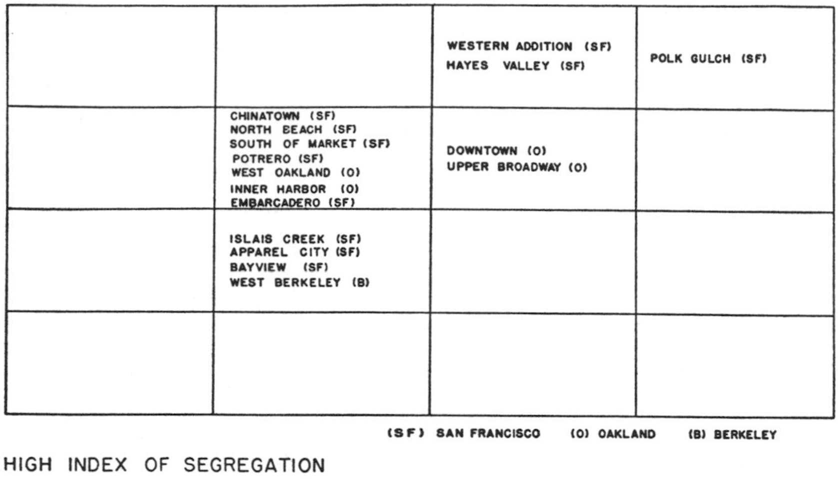

		WESTERN ADDITION (SF) HAYES VALLEY (SF)	POLK GULCH (SF)
	CHINATOWN (SF) NORTH BEACH (SF) SOUTH OF MARKET (SF) POTRERO (SF) WEST OAKLAND (O) INNER HARBOR (O) EMBARCADERO (SF)	DOWNTOWN (O) UPPER BROADWAY (O)	
	ISLAIS CREEK (SF) APPAREL CITY (SF) BAYVIEW (SF) WEST BERKELEY (B)		

(SF) SAN FRANCISCO   (O) OAKLAND   (B) BERKELEY

HIGH INDEX OF SEGREGATION

FIG. V-13.—Selected places representative of the social areas of the San Francisco Bay Region, 1950 (high index of segregation).

the social areas having low indexes of segregation and high indexes of segregation are given.

Human geographers, ecologists, city planners, and others may be interested in constructing a map like the one in Figure V-14, which shows the geographical location of the 1950 social areas of the San Francisco Bay Region.

ETHNIC GROUPS

We feel that the analysis of racial, nationality, and cultural groups which follows is necessary to complete the picture of the social structure of an urban area as that structure is revealed by the study of census tract statistics. First, the size of the major ethnic groups is given for the two time periods. Second, a measure of probable interaction between members of the same group and between members of different groups based on residential concentration is computed. Third, the distribution of the major ethnic groups in the social areas for both 1940 and 1950 is given. These three types of analysis, taken together, reveal the structure and change in the ethnic composition of the urban population under study, as well as permit the delineation of ethnic residential concentrations and the determination of the present status and recent changes in the social position of the ethnic groups. Any research worker interested in the place of ethnic groups in modern American society would certainly execute the following analysis.

Relative size of selected ethnic groups.—Table V-1 contains the number and percent of the population represented by the major groups in the Bay Region in 1940 and 1950. The native whites are the largest group, representing 77.1 percent of the population in 1940 and 72.8 percent in 1950. The Orientals are the next largest group in 1940, representing 3.2 percent of the population, followed by the Italians (3.0 percent) and the Negroes (1.5 percent). In

1950, however, the largest group, other than the native white group, are the Negroes, representing 8.3 percent of the population. The Mexicans are next (3.9 percent), followed by the Orientals (3.5 percent) and the Italians (1.9 percent).[9]

The increase in the number of Negroes from 17,286 in 1940 to 125,564 in 1950 accounted for an increase of 626.4 percent, the largest percentage change of any group. The Mexican group and Oriental group both had percentage increases in excess of the percentage increase for native whites. The Russians had a percentage increase of 10.1 percent, but the foreign-born white from Italy decreased by 14.2 percent. The most striking change from 1940 to 1950, in the relative sizes of the various groups, of course, is the influx of Negroes into the Bay Region. With these changes in the ethnic composition of the population in mind, we will now present an analysis of the residential concentration of the various groups.

TABLE V-1

NUMBER AND PERCENT OF THE POPULATION REPRESENTED BY SELECTED GROUPS
IN THE SAN FRANCISCO BAY REGION, 1940 AND 1950

Group	Number 1940	Percent 1940	Number 1950	Percent 1950	Number Change	Percent Change
Native whites ..	863,324	77.1	1,099,456	72.8	+236,132	+ 27.4
Negroes	17,286	1.5	125,564	8.3	+108,278	+626.4
Orientals	35,892	3.2	53,460	3.5	+ 17,568	+ 48.9
Russians	8,896	0.8	9,792	0.7	+ 806	+ 10.1
Italians	33,340	3.0	28,598	1.9	− 4,742	− 14.2
Mexicans*	12,820	1.1	59,172	3.9	+ 46,352	+361.6

* The 1940 and 1950 figures for Mexicans are not strictly comparable.

The index of isolation.—Ecological isolation is defined as the residential concentration of the members of a particular group with other members of the same group. Using the probability model constructed by Bell (1954) to measure spatial isolation, the P* scores and indexes of isolation (I_1) were computed for the Bay Region for 1940 and 1950.[10] P* is subject to direct interpretation as

[9] The 1940 figures for Mexicans are estimates based on the number of foreign-born white from Mexico. The 1950 figures for Mexicans are based on the number of persons with Spanish surnames. The census category "nonwhite, other races" is used to represent Orientals. Italians are census category "foreign-born white from Italy"; the Russians are "foreign-born white from the U.S.S.R."

[10] Formulas for the index of isolation (I_1) and P*:

$$I_1 = \frac{P^* - \dfrac{A}{B}}{1.00 - \dfrac{A}{B}} \quad \text{and} \quad P^* = \frac{1}{A} \sum_{i=1}^{k} \frac{a_i^2}{b_i}$$

where:

a_i = the number of individuals of group 1 in the *i*th census tract.

the probability of a randomly selected member of a particular group next meeting in his census tract another member of the same group. An assessment of the degree of residential concentration of a particular group is given by I_1, which is an index based on P*, but which is relative to the possible limits of P* in the urban area under study. An I_1 of 0 equals "no segregation" and an I_1 of 1.00 equals "complete segregation."

Table V-2 contains the P* scores, minimum possible values of P* (A/B), and the indexes of isolation (I_1) for selected groups in the Bay Region for 1940 and 1950. For example, the probability of a randomly selected native white next meeting another native white was .80 in 1940 and .77 in 1950. If the native whites had been homogeneously mixed with the rest of the population,[11] however, P* would have been .77, i.e., A/B, in 1940 and .73 in 1950. Setting A/B at 0, the native whites were slightly more isolated in 1950 ($I_1 = .17$) than in 1940 ($I_1 = .10$).

Comparing the other 1940 and 1950 indexes of isolation given in Table V-2, it can be seen that the spatial isolation of the Negroes increased from 1940 ($I_1 = .15$) to 1950 ($I_1 = .33$). An increase in the probability of a randomly selected Negro next meeting another Negro was expected to increase from 1940 (P* = .16) to 1950 (P* = .38) owing to the relative increase in the sheer number of Negroes. However, when each P* is made relative to the minimum possible P* in 1940 ($A/B = .02$) and in 1950 ($A/B = .08$), a large increase in the spatial isolation of the Negroes, as is shown by the above comparison of the I_1's, is still apparent.

The Orientals ($I_1 = .41$), more highly isolated than the Negroes in 1940, were somewhat less spatially isolated than the Negroes in 1950 (Orientals $I_1 = .28$). The Russians, Italians, and Mexicans were less concentrated residentially than the native whites in 1940 and 1950. Generally, the Italians, Russians, and Mexicans showed little change in their respective indexes of isolation from 1940 to 1950. The Russians were the least isolated group in 1940 ($I_1 = .01$) and in 1950 ($I_1 = .01$).

The group segregation ratio II.—A complete assessment of the ecological concentration of a given subordinate ethnic group requires some measure of the residential proximity of the group with other subordinate ethnic groups. For example, a measure reflecting the residential concentration of the Negroes alone only partially reflects the effective residential isolation of the Negroes, *if the Negroes live in areas characterized by other subordinate racial and nationality*

---

b_i = the total number of individuals in the ith tract.

k = the number of census tracts in the urban area under study.

$A = \sum_{i=1}^{k} a_i$ = the total number of group 1 in the urban area under study.

$B = \sum_{i=1}^{k} b_i$ = the total population of the urban area under study.

[11] As defined here, a group is homogeneously mixed with the remainder of the population if its proportion in each census tract equals its proportion in the region as a whole; i.e., if every $a_i/b_i = A/B$.

TABLE V-2

P* Scores, Minimum Values of P*, and Indexes of Isolation (I_1) for Selected Groups in the San Francisco Bay Region, 1940 and 1950

Group	P*		P* Min. = A/B		I_1	
	1940	1950	1940	1950	1940	1950
Native whites	.80	.77	.78	.73	.10	.17
Negroes	.16	.38	.02	.08	.15	.33
Orientals	.43	.31	.03	.04	.41	.28
Russians	.02	.02	.01	.01	.01	.01
Italians	.10	.06	.03	.02	.07	.04
Mexicans	.05	.07	.01	.04	.04	.03

groups. Another index was constructed to measure the probable interaction between members of one of the subordinate groups with the members of all the subordinate groups. R* is the probability of a random member of group 1 (one of the subordinate groups) next meeting another member of group 1 or a member of one of the other racial and nationality groups defined as subordinate.[12]

The group segregation ratio II, I_3, is an index based on R* and is designed to relate R* to its possible minimum for a given group in the urban area under study.[13] I_3 attains its maximum of 1.00 under conditions of "complete segregation" of group 1 when the probability of a randomly selected member of group 1 next meeting a member of group 1 or a member of group 2 (the other subordinate groups) is 1.00. I_3 attains its minimum value of 0 under conditions of

[12] The racial and nationality groups used here are suggested as a standard measure in all American cities. They are given later in the chapter devoted to computational procedures.

[13] Formulas for the Group Segregation Ratio II (I_3) and R*:

$$I_3 = \frac{R^* - \dfrac{A}{B - A'}}{1.00 - \dfrac{A}{B - A'}} \quad \text{and} \quad R^* = \frac{1}{A} \sum_{i=1}^{k} \frac{a_i (a_i + a_i')}{b_i}$$

where

a_i = the number of individuals of group 1, one of the subordinate groups, in the ith census tract.

a_i' = the total number of persons who are members of racial and nationality groups traditionally having subordinate status in American society in the ith tract minus the number of persons in group 1 in the ith tract.

b_i = the total number of individuals in the ith tract.

$A = \sum_{i=1}^{k} a_i$ = the total number of group 1, one of the subordinate groups, in the urban area under study.

$A' = \sum_{i=1}^{k} a_i'$ = the total number of the subordinate groups in the urban area under study minus the total number of persons in group 1.

$B = \sum_{i=1}^{k} b_i$ = the total population of the urban area under study.

"no segregation" of group 1 when the probability of a random member of group 1 next meeting another member of group 1 or a member of group 2 is $A/(B-A')$; that is, when all the members of the combined subordinate groups except group 1 are in one set of tracts, and all the members of group 1 are homogeneously mixed with the rest of the population in the remaining tracts.

Table V-3 contains the R* scores, the minimum values of R*, i.e., $A/(B-A')$, and the group segregation ratio II (I_3) for selected groups in the Bay Region for 1940 and 1950.[14] For example, the probability of an Oriental next meeting another Oriental or a member of one of the other subordinate groups was .54 in 1940 and .50 in 1950. Setting the minimum value of R* at o in each case (.04 for both 1940 and 1950), it can be determined that the Orientals were residentially concentrated with the subordinate groups to about the same degree in 1940 ($I_3 = .52$) and in 1950 ($I_3 = .48$). The Negroes were more highly concentrated with the subordinate groups in 1950 ($I_3 = .47$) than they were in 1940 ($I_3 = .31$). The residential segregation of the Mexicans with all the subordinate groups stayed about the same in 1940 ($I_3 = .22$) and 1950 ($I_3 = .23$). The concentration of the Italians and the Russians with the subordinate groups increased very slightly.

TABLE V-3

R* Scores, Minimum Values of R*, and the Group Segregation Ratios II (I_3) for Selected Groups in the San Francisco Bay Region, 1940 and 1950

Group	R* 1940	R* 1950	R* Min. $= \frac{A}{B-A'}$ 1940	R* Min. $= \frac{A}{B-A'}$ 1950	I_3 1940	I_3 1950
Negroes	.32	.52	.02	.09	.31	.47
Orientals	.54	.50	.04	.04	.52	.48
Russians	.14	.19	.01	.01	.13	.18
Italians	.20	.24	.03	.02	.17	.22
Mexicans	.23	.27	.01	.05	.22	.23

Comparing the relative degree of residential concentration of the different groups, it can be seen from Table V-3 that in 1940 the Orientals were the most highly concentrated with the subordinate groups ($I_3 = .52$), the Negroes were next most highly concentrated ($I_3 = .31$); next were the Mexicans ($I_3 = .22$), the Italians ($I_3 = .17$), and the Russians ($I_3 = .13$). In 1950 the Negroes ($I_3 = .47$) were residentially associated with the subordinate groups to about the same degree as the Orientals ($I_3 = .48$). The Mexicans ($I_3 = .23$), the Italians ($I_3 = .22$), and the Russians ($I_3 = .18$) remained less segregated with the subordinate groups than the Negroes and Orientals.

The group segregation ratio I (I_2).—Another measure of the probable interaction of two groups is the group segregation ratio I (I_2). This index differs from I_3 in that it measures the neighborhood association of group 1 with the combined subordinate groups *when group 1 is not one of the subordinate groups.*

[14] The R* scores and I_3 scores given by Bell (1954: 362) do not exactly correspond with those given here, since the "combined subordinate groups" category nas been more inclusively defined in this report.

Q* is the probability that the next person a random individual of group 1 will meet is from group 2.[15]

Defining group 1 as native whites and group 2 as all the subordinate groups, in 1940 the probability of a randomly selected native white next meeting a member of the subordinate groups in his census tract was .10 (Q* = .10). In 1950 a randomly selected native white would meet a Negro, Oriental, Mexican, Italian, or a member of one of the other subordinate groups sixteen times out of his next one hundred meetings in his census tract (Q* = .16).

The minimum value of Q* is 0, which is achieved when no census tract has individuals from both groups; the maximum value is $A'/(A+A')$, which is achieved when each census tract contains either no members of either group or only members of both groups, and these in the fixed proportion A/A'. Returning to our comparison of the residential proximity of the native whites to the combined subordinate groups in 1940 and 1950, Q* would achieve its minimum value of 0 when the native whites were in one set of census tracts in which there were no members of the subordinate groups, and when the remaining tracts contained all the members of the subordinate groups but no native whites. Thus, a small value of Q* indicates complete lack of residential association between native whites and the combined subordinate groups. The maximum value of Q*, on the other hand, is achieved when the native whites are homogeneously mixed with the members of the subordinate groups in one set of tracts with the rest of the population in the remaining tracts; in 1940 the possible maximum value of Q* was .14, and in 1950 it was .22.

Placing the actual Q*'s in a relative position with respect to their possible minimum and maximum by setting Q*'s maximum $A'/(A+A')$ at 1.00, we have the group segregation ratio I (I_2). For the native whites in 1940, I_2 was .73 and in 1950 I_2 was .72, indicating that the native whites had about the same degree of residential association with the subordinate groups at both times. I_2 scores of .73 and .72, of course, indicate that, relative to the limits set by the proportion of groups 1 and 2 in the population, there was considerable residential association between the native whites and the members of the combined subordinate groups.

Social area distributions of the selected groups.—The social area distributions of the selected groups are given for 1940 in Figure V-15. The numbers in the social areas represent the percent of each group contained in the social area. Notice that the distributions of each group in the various social areas are different. The Mexicans had the largest percentage of their group contained in the social areas with social rank less than 50 (73.1 percent); the Italians were next most highly concentrated in the lower social rank social areas (68.6 percent), followed by the Negroes (62.3 percent), the Orientals (52.5 percent),

[15] Formulas for the Group Segregation Ratio I (I_2) and Q*:

$$I_2 = Q^* \left/ \frac{A'}{A+A'} \right. \quad \text{and} \quad Q^* = \frac{1}{A} \sum_{i=1}^{k} \frac{a_i\, a_i'}{b_i}$$

where all the terms have the same definitions as those used in R* except that a_i' (thus A') refers to *all* the members of the racial, nationality, and cultural groups considered subordinate and a_i is *not* one of the subordinate groups.

	1.7	14.4	1.9
.4	16.6	13.7	.9
16.0	27.4	5.7	1.1
	.2	0	

NEGROES

	7.2	29.0	6.2
.3	37.3	5.8	2.2
1.4	6.3	3.0	1.3
	0	0	

ORIENTALS

	8.4	9.5	2.7
3.2	27.4	9.4	1.4
7.9	21.5	7.2	1.0
	.2	.2	

ITALIANS

	6.8	9.0	2.0
4.7	26.6	10.4	1.3
16.4	18.0	3.2	.8
	.6	.2	

MEXICANS

	2.3	21.0	7.2
5.1	13.1	28.5	5.8
1.0	7.2	6.5	2.2
	0	.1	

RUSSIANS

	2.6	9.4	6.9
.8	13.5	18.1	5.6
3.2	17.2	15.1	6.7
	.2	.7	

NATIVE WHITES

URBANIZATION (HIGH / LOW)

1D	2D	3D	4D
1C	2C	3C	4C
1B	2B	3B	4B
1A	2A	3A	4A

SOCIAL RANK (LOW / HIGH)

STANFORD SURVEY RESEARCH FACILITY

FIG. V-15.—Distribution of selected groups in the social areas of the San Francisco Bay Region, 1940.

the native whites (37.5 percent), and the Russians (28.7 percent). Only the Russians (71.3 percent) and the native whites (62.5 percent) had more than half of their group living in social areas having social rank scores in excess of 50.

The most urban (lowest family status) group was the Oriental, with 88.0 percent of Orientals residing in social areas with urbanization scores of 50 or more in 1940. The next most urban group in 1940 was the Russians, with 83.0 percent of the group located in the higher urbanization social areas. The percentages of the other groups contained in the higher urbanization social areas were 62.0 percent for the Italians, 60.8 percent for the Mexicans, 56.9 percent for the native whites, and 49.6 percent for the Negroes, the latter being the least urbanized group in 1940.

Figure V-16 contains the 1950 social area distributions of the selected groups. Generally, all of the groups shifted somewhat into social areas of higher social rank, and, although less marked, most of the groups shifted into social areas of lower urbanization (higher family status) from 1940 to 1950. The largest relative increase into the highest social rank social areas 4A, 4B, 4C, and 4D occurred in the Russian group, while the Negroes' proportion in the highest social rank social areas increased the least of any group (from 3.9 percent in 1940 to 4.6 percent in 1950).

The relative position of the selected groups with respect to the dimensions of social rank and urbanization remained about the same in 1950 as they were in 1940. In 1950, however, the Negroes had the largest percentage (55.7 percent) in social areas having social rank scores less than 50. The Mexicans had the next largest percentage (45.8 percent) in these lower social rank social areas. Then came the Orientals (39.7 percent), the Italians (33.3 percent), the native whites (18.6 percent), and the Russians (15.8 percent).

The differences in the percentages of the groups in the four highest social rank social areas are even more striking. The Russians had the largest percentage of their group (48.7 percent) in the highest social rank social areas 4A, 4B, 4C, and 4D, which have social rank scores of 75 or higher.[16] The native whites had a smaller percentage (36.0 percent) of their group in the highest social rank social areas than the Russians, but a larger percentage than any other group. The Orientals had the next largest percentage (23.7 percent), the Italians next (23.0 percent), the Mexicans next (14.2 percent); and finally, the Negroes had the smallest percentage (4.6 percent) in the highest social rank social areas.

The most urban group in 1950 was, as in 1940, the Orientals with 83.7 percent of the group living in social areas characterized by higher urbanization, i.e., social areas with urbanization scores of 50 or more. The Russians remained

---

[16] This finding can be compared with a finding of Broom and Shevky (1949). They found in 1940 that the foreign-born whites from the U.S.S.R. in Los Angeles County were concentrated in the higher urbanization social areas, but were distributed over most of the range of the social rank continuum. (It should be pointed out that the "foreign-born whites from the U.S.S.R.," while predominantly Jewish in Los Angeles, composes to that extent only one segment of the total Jewish population. Also, the "foreign-born whites from the U.S.S.R." probably contains fewer Jews in the Bay Region than in Los Angeles.)

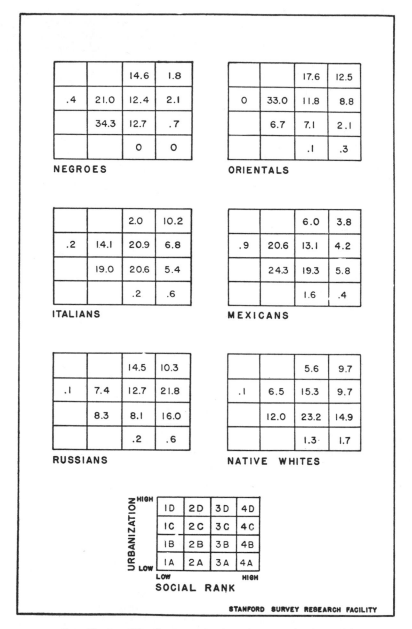

FIG. V-16.—Distribution of selected groups in the social areas of the San Francisco Bay Region, 1950.

the next most urban group with 66.8 percent of their group residing in the higher urbanization social areas; and the Italians were next with 54.2 percent living in these social areas. The Negroes had 52.3 percent living in the higher urbanization social areas, while the Mexicans had 48.6 percent and the native whites had 46.9 percent. While the Negroes had the largest percentage living in the lower urbanization social areas in 1940, the native whites had the largest percentage in 1950. The percentage of each of the groups living in the higher urbanization social areas decreased from 1940 to 1950 for every group except the Negroes and the Italians. With respect to urbanization the general pattern of the social area distribution of the various groups and the differences among them remained about the same in 1950 as in 1940.

   Geographical distribution of the selected groups.—In addition to the social area analysis of the ethnic groups given above, many researchers will want to continue the analysis by locating the ethnic communities geographically. Figure V-17 contains a map showing the geographical distribution of the selected groups in 1950. Each symbol represents a census tract which contained a greater than average proportion of the subordinate group members; i.e., a census tract with an index of segregation in excess of 20.7. In addition, each symbol indicates which

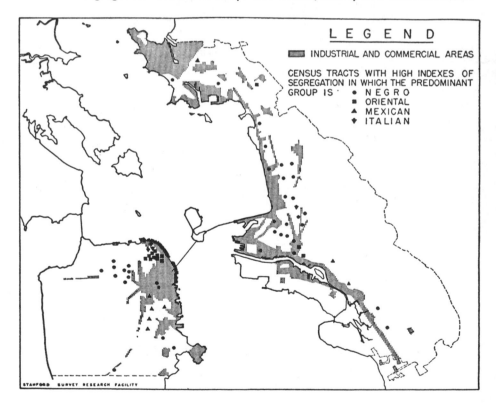

FIG. V-17.—Geographical distribution of the census tracts with high indexes of segregation with the predominant group indicated.

one of the subordinate groups living in the "segregated" tract represented the largest proportion of the total tract population. For example, segregated tracts in which the largest proportion of any of the particular subordinate groups was Negro were designated "Negro tracts." Segregated tracts in which the predominant subordinate group was Oriental were designated "Oriental tracts," etc. As can be seen from Figure V-17, of the sixty-three segregated tracts there were thirty-eight designated Negro tracts, thirteen were designated Oriental tracts, eight were designated Mexican tracts, and four were designated Italian tracts. No other one of the nationality or racial groups considered subordinate predominated in any of the segregated tracts.

Notice in Figure V-17 the decided tendency for the segregated tracts to be located near the Bay, in or near areas which are mainly industrial or commercial. Also notice the geographical clustering of segregated tracts having the same predominant ethnic group.

VI. COMPUTATIONAL PROCEDURES

The social position of a census tract population as determined within this framework is a function of three basic dimensions: social rank, urbanization, and segregation.[1] The position of a tract with respect to social rank and urbanization is shown graphically when plotted on a system of rectangular co-ordinates, with social rank as the horizontal axis and urbanization as the vertical axis. In order to group tracts with similar social positions with respect to social rank and urbanization, the plane in which a given number of tracts is thus plotted is segmented. Each segment is called a social area. Tracts plotted in one social area comprise a single type in the classification. The third dimension, segregation, is introduced to distinguish differences among tracts in a given social area as defined by social rank and urbanization. With the exception of one special tabulation (Spanish surname data) the data required are given in the following sources:

, U.S. Bureau of the Census, *Population and Housing, Statistics for Census Tracts*, 1940; and U.S. Bureau of the Census, *United States Census of Population, Census Tract Statistics*, 1950, Volume III (series P-D).

I. For each census tract compile the basic data and compute the ratios for the indexes of social rank, urbanization, and segregation. Compute the standard scores and combine these into index scores as indicated below:

A. *Social Rank Components*

    1. *Occupation ratio* (total number of craftsmen . . . , operatives . . . , and laborers . . . per 1,000 employed persons). (In 1950 add males and females in these occupational categories.)

      a) Add:
        (1) "Craftsmen, foremen, and kindred workers"
        (2) "Operatives and kindred workers"
        (3) "Laborers" ("Laborers, except mine" in 1950 census)

      b) Subtract the total number of persons with "Occupation not reported" from the total number of persons "Employed" ["Employed (exc. on pub. emerg. works)" in 1940 census].

      c) Divide the total number of craftsmen . . . , operatives . . . , and laborers by the above difference.

      d) Multiply the above quotient by 1,000.

    2. *Occupation standard score*[2]

      a) Substitute in standard score formula:
        Occupation score $= 100 - [x(r - o)]$

---

[1] Alternative designations for the three basic dimensions are *economic status, family status*, and *ethnic status*, respectively.

[2] See Appendix B for a discussion of the standard scores. All scores composing the index of social rank and the index of urbanization have been standardized to their ranges for the Los Angeles Area in 1940.

where
$x = .1336898$
$o = o$
$r =$ occupation ratio for each census tract

3. *Education ratio* (number of persons who have completed no more than grade school per 1,000 persons 25 years old and over)

   a) Add number of persons 25 years old and over who have had only eight years of schooling or less.

   b) Subtract the total number of persons with "School years not reported" from the total number of "Persons 25 years old and over."

   c) Divide the total number of persons completing only elementary school or less by the above difference.

   d) Multiply the quotient by 1,000.

4. *Education standard score*

   a) Substitute in standard score formula:
   Education score $= 100 - [x(r - o)]$
      where
      $x = .1298701$
      $o = 130$
      $r =$ education ratio for each census tract

5. *Social rank index*

   a) Compute a simple average of the occupation and education standard scores. The average is the index of social rank.

B. *Urbanization Components*

   1. *Fertility ratio* (number of children under 5 years per 1,000 females age 15 through 44)

      a) Record total number of persons "Under 5 years." (For 1950 add the number of males and females "Under 5 years.")

      b) Add the number of females in the age range 15 through 44.

      c) Divide the total number of children under 5 by the total number of females age 15 through 44.

      d) Multiply the quotient by 1,000.

   2. *Fertility standard score*

      a) Substitute in standard score formula:
      Fertility score $= 100 - [x(r - o)]$
         where
         $x = .1661130$
         $o = 9$
         $r =$ fertility ratio for each census tract

   3. *Women in the labor force ratio* (the number of females in the labor force per 1,000 females 14 years old and over)

      a) Record number of females "14 years old and over" who are in the "Labor force."

    b) Divide the above by the total number of females "14 years old and over."

    c) Multiply the quotient by 1,000. (In 1940 the percent of women in the labor force was given as a summary figure. If 1940 data are used, multiply by 10 to convert to ratio.)

4. *Women in the labor force standard score*

    a) Substitute in standard score formula:
    Women in the labor force score $= x(r - o)$
      where

        $x = .2183406$
        $o = 86$
        $r =$ women in the labor force ratio for each census tract

5. *Single-family detached dwelling units ratio* (the number of single-family dwelling units per 1,000 dwelling units of all types)[3]

    a) Record number of "1 dwelling unit, detached (includes trailers)" in 1950 census. (The definition in 1940 was "1-family detached" dwelling units.)

    b) Divide by total of "All dwelling units."

    c) Multiply the quotient by 1,000.

6. *Single-family detached dwelling units standard score*

    a) Substitute in standard score formula:
    S.F.D.U. score $= 100 - [x(r - o)]$
      where

        $x = .1006441$
        $o = 6$
        $r =$ single-family detached dwelling units ratio

7. *Urbanization index*

    a) Compute a simple average of the fertility, women in the labor force, and single-family dwelling units standard scores. The average is the index of urbanization.

C. *The Index of Segregation*

    1. Add the number of persons designated "Negro"; "Other Races"; and "foreign-born white" from "Poland," "Czechoslovakia," "Hungary," "Yugoslavia," "U.S.S.R.," "Lithuania," "Finland," "Rumania," "Greece," "Italy," "Other Europe,"[4] "Asia," "French Canada," "Mexico," and "Other America."[5] In 1940 the comparable categories

---

[3] An error appears in Shevky and Williams (1949: 69) and Bell (1953: 41) in which occupied dwellings are reported as the base of the ratio. The correct measure used was *all* dwellings.

[4] Include "foreign-born white from Other Europe" only if the category contains mostly foreign-born white from southern and eastern Europe.

[5] For cities in Arizona, California, Colorado, New Mexico, and Texas the number of white persons with Spanish surnames can be used instead of the number of foreign-born white from Mexico and Other America. A special tabulation must be requested

were the number of persons designated "Negro"; "Other Races"; and "foreign-born white" from "Poland," "Czechoslovakia," "Hungary," "Yugoslavia," "Russia (U.S.S.R.)," "Lithuania," "Finland," "Rumania," "Greece," "Italy," "Spain and Portugal," "Other Europe," "Asia," "French Canada," "Mexico,"[6] "Cuba and Other West Indies," and "Central and South America."

2. Divide the above sum by the total population in each tract.

3. Multiply the above quotient by 100 to obtain the index of segregation for each census tract.[7]

II. Construction of the Social Areas

A. *Divisions in the Index of Social Rank.* Divide the census tracts into four groups on the basis of their scores on the index of social rank. Group tracts together having social rank scores of 0 to 24, 25 to 49, 50 to 74, and 75 to 100, respectively. Designate these groups of tracts as social areas of the order 1, 2, 3, and 4, respectively.

B. *Divisions in the Index of Urbanization.* Divide the census tracts into four groups on the basis of their scores on the index of urbanization. Group together tracts having urbanization scores of 0 to 24, 25 to 49, 50 to 74, and 75 to 100. Designate these groups of tracts as social areas of the order A, B, C, and D, respectively. Combining these divisions in the index of social rank, there are sixteen possible social areas. These are designated 1A, 1B, 1C, 2A, . . . 4D (see Fig. IV-1, p. 26).

---

from the U.S. Census Bureau in order to obtain the Spanish surname data in each census tract. If Spanish surname data are used, then the number of native whites in each census tract must be reduced by the number of native whites with Spanish surnames for the computation of I_1 and I_2 for the native whites.

[6] For 1940 the total number of persons classified as "foreign-born from Mexico" was converted into an estimate of the total number of Mexicans by establishing the proportion of the total population in the county for which the analysis was to take place represented by Mexicans in 1930, which is given in the 1930 census bulletins. The total number of Mexicans in 1940 was estimated by assuming they represented the same proportion of the total population in 1940 as in 1930. The number of foreign-born whites from Mexico was inflated for each tract so that the total number of Mexicans in 1940 equaled the total number estimated by the above procedure.

[7] Computational procedures for the index of isolation (I_1) and the group segregation ratios (I_2 and I_3) will not be presented here, since complete formulas were given in Chapter V. If the researcher prefers to use the alternative designations for the three constructs, no change is required in the computational procedures as given for the indexes of social rank and segregation. In the case of the index of urbanization it is only necessary to subtract each score from 100 (or to use the alternate standard score formula for the variables fertility, women in the labor force, and single-family dwellings). If this is done, also invert the letter designations for the social areas with respect to urbanization, so that the social area groupings will remain unchanged and named as before. That is, the *highest* family status social areas will be of the order A, just as the *lowest* urbanization social areas are now of the order A.

C. *Divisions in the Index of Segregation.* Divide the census tracts into two groups on the basis of their scores on the index of segregation. Select as the cutting point the percent of the total population of the urban area represented by the combined racial and nationality groups considered subordinate. Those tracts having more than the average proportion of the combined subordinate groups designate "segregated" tracts; those tracts having less than the average proportion of the combined subordinate groups designate "not segregated." Thus, there are thirty-two possible groupings of census tracts into social areas: 1A, 1B, 1C, 1D, 2A, . . . 4D and 1AS, 1BS, 1CS, 1DS, 2AS, . . . 4DS.[8]

[8] It is suggested that a visual representation of the social area distribution be obtained also by plotting the census tracts in a scattergram using the indexes of social rank and urbanization as the horizontal and vertical co-ordinates. Segregated tracts can be given a distinguishing symbol (see Fig. V-2, p. 30, and Fig. V-3, p. 31).

VII. SUMMARY AND CONCLUSION

In an earlier contribution a typology was developed by Shevky and Williams (1949) for the description and analysis of certain aspects of the social structure of the city. The basic elements of this typology were three constructs—social rank, urbanization, and segregation—and the unit of analysis was the census tract. In this volume the theoretical considerations which led to the formation of these constructs, and to the construction of their respective indexes out of the available urban demographic data, were derived with the aid of hypotheses from a historical analysis of the modes of expansion and transformation of the whole containing society. The constructs, social rank, urbanization, and segregation, were developed in relation to sociological theory and available empirical materials. We have argued that these constructs could be interpreted in terms of the broader implications of these same theoretical formulations and empirical materials.

We have here traced the interconnections of a still wider range of theory and empirical data in relation to what we consider to be the three basic factors of urban differentiation than was possible in the original study by Shevky and Williams. Consequently, the present formulation represents an advance over our earlier position, but an advance necessitated by the logic of the initial reasoning, and closely articulated with the elements of the earlier work.

In addition, we have here proposed several minor revisions of the original typology which increase its precision as an instrument for the comparative study of urban internal differentiation. The use of the typology has been illustrated by a presentation of its application to the 1940 and 1950 census data for one metropolitan region, the San Francisco Bay Region. In order to facilitate comparative studies by other researchers, detailed compilational and computational procedures have also been given.

We believe that the formulation of social trends in relation to current differentiating factors, including the typology based on these factors, in its present form has sufficient coherence, internal consistency, and specificity for us to make these further claims for it:

a) It is simple in statement.
b) It serves as an organizing principle.
c) It is theory-linked; it permits the derivation of testable propositions.
d) It is precise in its specifications; it permits observer agreement.
e) It represents a continuity with similar formulations which it aims to replace.

APPENDIXES

APPENDIX A

Census Tract	Identifying Place Name	Social Rank 1940	Social Rank 1950	Urbanization 1940	Urbanization 1950	Segregation 1940	Segregation 1950	Social Area 1940	Social Area 1950
Tracts in the City of San Francisco									
A–1	North Beach, Embarcadero ...	25	47	66	63	32.0	25.0	2CS	2CS*
A–2	North Beach, Russian Hill ...	79	88	82	82	10.7	10.3	4D	4D
A–3	North Beach, Russian Hill ...	43	58	75	71	30.5	30.8	2DS	3CS
A–4	North Beach, Telegraph Hill .	35	51	72	67	36.9	36.9	2CS	3CS
A–5	North Beach	26	43	67	51	54.4	66.5	2CS	2CS
A–6	North Beach	32	42	77	65	60.6	73.1	2DS	2CS
A–7	North Beach, Russian Hill ...	68	75	82	74	31.7	54.1	3DS	4CS
A–8	Polk Gulch	65	75	82	81	14.2	20.5	3DS	4D
A–9	Polk Gulch	65	76	89	79	12.8	31.2	3D	4DS
A–10	Polk Gulch	74	76	99	97	6.2	15.5	3D	4D
A–11	Nob Hill	80	83	88	85	28.5	36.8	4DS	4DS
A–12	Nob Hill	88	91	102	104	5.3	8.7	4D	4D
A–13	Chinatown	59	63	78	78	91.4	83.1	3DS	3DS
A–14	Chinatown	37	37	58	58	99.3	99.1	2CS	2CS
A–15	Chinatown	44	46	66	63	91.5	92.4	2CS	2CS
A–16	Embarcadero	35	45	80	58	49.4	64.3	2DS	2CS
A–17	Downtown Commercial	72	77	103	97	21.0	28.2	3DS	4DS
A–18	Downtown, Nob Hill	89	89	105	104	4.1	5.6	4D	4D
A–19	Downtown Commercial	78	82	103	103	4.8	6.0	4D	4D
A–20	Downtown Commercial	73	80	98	101	6.3	7.3	3D	4D
A–21	Downtown Commercial	75	80	98	99	6.3	6.3	4D	4D
A–22	Downtown Commercial	67	69	99	100	9.9	9.4	3D	3D
A–23	Civic Center	65	67	94	94	7.5	9.5	3D	3D
B–1	Marina, Fort Mason	87	89	76	82	8.0	9.6	4D	4D
B–2	Marina	85	88	73	80	8.5	10.3	4C	4D
B–3	Marina	74	80	71	73	13.3	13.0	3CS	4C
B–4	Marina	66	77	77	78	18.1	18.5	3DS	4D
B–5	Pacific Heights	69	77	79	80	16.4	15.7	3DS	4D
B–6	Pacific Heights	92	96	90	91	6.6	6.8	4D	4D
B–7	Pacific Heights	93	96	77	78	8.4	8.5	4D	4D
B–8	Presidio Heights	80	87	70	77	9.8	18.3	4C	4D
B–9	Pacific Heights	76	76	76	82	15.2	30.9	4DS	4DS
B–10	Pacific Heights	82	83	88	91	12.6	19.0	4D	4D
D–1	Richmond, Presidio Terrace ..	63	67	61	64	9.9	12.3	3C	3C
D–2	Richmond	68	77	68	67	7.5	10.8	3C	4C
E–1	Sea Cliff	93	93	53	42	8.3	9.5	4C	4B
E–2	Park-Presidio	64	75	64	57	7.6	10.3	3C	4C

* S indicates that the census tract was designated segregated. A tract was designated segregated if more than 12.8 percent in 1940 and 20.7 percent in 1950 of the tract population was represented by members of the combined subordinate groups.

Census Tract	Identifying Place Name	Social Rank		Urbani- zation		Segre- gation		Social Area	
		1940	1950	1940	1950	1940	1950	1940	1950
E–3	Park-Presidio	71	78	64	67	9.1	10.5	3C	4C
G–1	Park-Presidio	74	79	62	62	7.7	12.2	3C	4C
G–2	Park-Presidio	72	78	59	60	9.3	12.9	3C	4C
G–3	Outer Richmond	75	80	59	50	7.0	11.4	4C	4C
G–4	Outer Richmond, Vista del Mar	71	79	59	45	5.8	10.3	3C	4B
H–1	Richmond	54	68	68	68	9.5	13.3	3C	3C
H–2	Richmond	67	75	67	63	8.5	13.5	3C	4C
J–1	Western Addition (Geary-California)	72	68	93	94	8.8	16.9	3D	3D
J–2	Western Addition (Geary-California)	70	68	82	78	46.1	67.4	3DS	3DS
J–3	Western Addition (Geary-California)	57	56	67	73	28.7	67.7	3CS	3CS
J–4	Laurel Heights	68	75	67	69	20.1	36.6	3CS	4CS
J–5	Lone Mountain	62	77	66	64	10.7	20.0	3C	4C
J–6	Western Addition (Geary-California)	54	55	82	75	51.7	75.2	3DS	3DS
J–7	Western Addition (Fulton-Geary)	51	58	75	77	22.2	51.5	3DS	3DS
J–8	Western Addition (Fulton-Geary)	55	54	77	81	36.9	65.3	3DS	3DS
J–9	Western Addition (Fulton-Geary)	59	61	83	81	8.5	18.9	3D	3D
J–10	Western Addition (Fulton-Geary)	38	45	71	65	21.3	48.3	2CS	2CS
J–11	Hayes Valley, Civic Center ...	56	63	76	85	7.1	18.5	3D	3D
J–12	Hayes Valley	54	59	73	79	13.2	39.7	3CS	3DS
J–13	Hayes Valley	60	66	76	78	10.0	19.6	3D	3D
J–14	Haight-Ashbury	67	74	80	80	8.9	14.5	3D	3D
J–15	Haight-Ashbury	56	67	74	80	7.7	12.9	3C	3D
J–16	Haight-Fillmore	55	63	72	74	7.3	17.2	3C	3C
J–17	Haight-Fillmore	54	64	82	79	7.6	17.1	3D	3D
J–18	Haight-Fillmore	46	55	73	66	8.2	13.4	2C	3C
J–19	Buena Vista, Corona Heights..	61	68	67	66	7.1	9.4	3C	3C
J–20	Buena Vista, Haight-Ashbury, Ashbury Heights	64	73	65	72	7.2	9.6	3C	3C
K–1	South of Market, Embarcadero	38	46	75	69	18.7	18.9	2DS	2C
K–2	South of Market	42	39	80	71	14.3	18.6	2DS	2C
K–3	South of Market	28	31	63	67	29.1	46.4	2CS	2CS
K–4	South of Market	19	22	60	58	35.8	60.2	1CS	1CS
K–6	Mission, Potrero	25	32	62	68	20.2	40.0	2CS	2CS
L–1	Potrero	22	38	55	48	28.0	28.8	1CS	2BS
L–2	Potrero	29	37	57	59	16.4	29.6	2CS	2CS
L–3	Potrero, Bernal	33	40	62	61	13.9	22.8	2CS	2CS
L–4	Islais Creek, Apparel City, Portola Heights	16	41	49	36	23.5	33.6	1BS	2BS
L–5	Bayview, Hunter's Point	22	44	42	37	23.4	36.3	1BS	2BS
M–1	Bernal Heights, Peralta Heights	25	40	35	46	14.7	19.7	2BS	2B
M–2	Bernal Heights	30	38	56	51	15.5	21.4	2CS	2CS
M–3	Bernal Heights	35	48	61	58	9.8	16.1	2C	2C
M–4	Bernal, Holly Park	32	46	49	43	11.3	15.7	2B	2B

Census Tract	Identifying Place Name	Social Rank 1940	Social Rank 1950	Urbani-zation 1940	Urbani-zation 1950	Segre-gation 1940	Segre-gation 1950	Social Area 1940	Social Area 1950
M–5	Bayshore, Portola	29	50	42	40	17.9	16.4	2BS	3B
M–6	Outer Mission (Excelsior) ...	26	43	56	33	17.6	19.9	2CS	2B
M–7	Outer Mission, Mission Terrace	38	51	49	40	11.1	16.0	2B	3B
M–8	Outer Mission (Cayuga)	37	50	44	34	11.0	12.1	2B	3B
M–9	Outer Mission, Crocker-Amazon	37	47	40	33	7.8	30.8	2B	2BS
M–10	Outer Mission (McLaren Park)	36	58	34	33	13.9	11.9	2BS	3B
M–11	Visitacion Valley	28	46	39	41	15.3	17.4	2BS	2B
N–1	Mission (Market–17th)	32	39	73	72	12.6	20.2	2C	2C
N–2	Mission (Market–17th)	47	57	82	71	6.7	9.7	2D	3C
N–3	Mission (Market–17th)	44	54	75	69	8.1	13.5	2D	3C
N–4	East of Twin Peaks, Eureka Valley	56	70	50	56	6.2	10.0	3C	3C
N–5	Eureka Valley	46	58	54	58	6.1	8.7	2C	3C
N–6	Mission (17th–22d), Eureka Valley	51	62	69	64	6.6	9.0	3C	3C
N–7	Mission (17th–22d)	44	58	71	72	6.8	9.9	2C	3C
N–8	Mission (17th–22d)	35	46	71	72	9.6	14.2	2C	2C
N–9	Mission (22d–Army)	38	50	72	76	8.9	14.4	2C	3D
N–10	Mission (22d–Army)	47	56	68	65	7.4	13.2	2C	3C
N–11	Mission (22d–Army), Dolores Heights	47	59	60	59	5.1	11.8	2C	3C
N-12	Mission (22d–Army), Noe Valley	45	58	59	55	5.3	7.8	2C	3C
N–13	Mission (Army–30th), Diamond Heights	34	52	36	29	11.5	11.2	2B	3B
N–14	Mission (Army–30th)	44	52	65	56	5.5	10.5	2C	3C
N–15	Fairmount–Glen Park	38	53	45	44	6.7	11.1	2B	3B
O–1	Mount Sutro–Parnassus Heights	72	75	67	72	8.3	11.9	3C	4C
O–2	Sunset	64	73	61	65	4.8	7.4	3C	3C
O–3	Sunset, Forest Hills, Golden Gate Heights	74	83	47	39	4.3	6.6	3B	4B
O–4	West of Twin Peaks, West Portal, Laguna Honda	83	88	47	45	3.3	5.8	4B	4B
O–5	West of Twin Peaks, Sunny-side, Miraloma Park	50	67	44	33	6.5	8.0	3B	3B
O–6	West of Twin Peaks, Westwood Highland, Westwood Park..	80	76	37	31	3.5	6.2	4B	4B
O–7	West of Twin Peaks, Balboa Terrace, Lakeside, Ingleside Terrace, St. Francis Wood..	89	92	35	30	3.9	6.3	4B	4B
O–8	Ocean View, Merced Heights..	43	63	44	31	7.4	12.5	2B	3B
O–9	Ingleside, San Miguel	41	57	43	38	6.2	15.2	2B	3B
P–1	Sunset	67	76	48	41	4.3	8.9	3B	4B
P–2	Sunset	70	78	39	43	3.5	6.9	3B	4B
P–3	Parkside, Stonestown, Park-Merced, Lakeshore	67	86	36	36	4.2	4.9	3B	4B
Q–1	Outer Sunset	62	78	40	40	4.5	7.0	3B	4B

Census Tract	Identifying Place Name	Social Rank 1940	Social Rank 1950	Urbanization 1940	Urbanization 1950	Segregation 1940	Segregation 1950	Social Area 1940	Social Area 1950
	Tracts in the City of Oakland								
1	East of Berkeley, Claremont District	92	99	52	32	10.4	5.0	4C	4B
2	North Oakland, Rockridge ...	84	90	47	44	2.6	4.1	4B	4B
3	North Oakland, Temescal	60	69	48	48	8.7	10.8	3B	3B
4	North Oakland, Temescal	66	75	52	55	6.5	8.4	3C	4C
5	North Oakland, Temescal	58	67	52	52	6.7	12.4	3C	3C
6	North Oakland, Golden Gate District	49	55	49	52	6.8	23.7	2B	3CS
7	North Oakland, Golden Gate District	32	47	43	51	14.0	42.2	2BS	2CS
8	Central Oakland, Temescal...	39	51	50	52	17.3	26.4	2CS	3CS
9	Central Oakland, Temescal...	57	66	53	57	8.0	10.1	3C	3C
10	Central Oakland, Temescal ...	46	61	63	64	13.6	29.6	2CS	3CS
11	Upper Broadway	55	59	67	75	22.7	47.4	3CS	3DS
12	Upper Broadway	56	58	71	69	8.2	23.1	3C	3CS
13	Upper Broadway	49	51	70	73	7.3	15.3	2C	3C
14	West Oakland	35	38	42	58	25.9	75.6	2BS	2CS
15	West Oakland, Outer Harbor	18	33	33	46	49.5	86.0	1BS	2BS
16	West Oakland	28	36	47	54	35.1	84.0	2BS	2CS
17	West Oakland	35	37	57	67	21.1	74.4	2CS	2CS
18	West Oakland, Downtown ...	39	40	69	69	12.2	43.9	2C	2CS
19	Downtown Commercial	50	56	86	82	8.0	10.7	3D	3D
20	Downtown Commercial	43	38	84	71	16.9	31.2	2DS	2CS
21	West Oakland, Inner Harbor..	16	25	39	46	55.2	82.3	1BS	2BS
22	Downtown Commercial, Inner Harbor	28	28	47	44	43.2	61.9	2BS	2BS
23	Downtown Commercial	48	45	70	71	50.9	58.4	2CS	2CS
24	Peralta, Inner Harbor	46	49	59	52	49.3	45.9	2CS	2CS
25	East Lake, Inner Harbor	36	45	55	63	9.7	18.2	2C	2C
26	East Lake	55	61	64	67	4.3	9.3	3C	3C
27	East Lake	70	74	76	79	4.5	5.5	3D	3D
28	Peralta, Lake Merritt	79	80	97	96	3.7	8.3	4D	4D
29	Downtown Commercial	76	76	93	89	4.4	7.8	4D	4D
30	Upper Broadway	73	81	68	74	6.4	8.0	3C	4C
31	Grand Avenue	88	90	79	80	4.4	6.1	4D	4D
32	Trestle Glen	85	87	65	65	3.8	7.0	4C	4C
33	Park Boulevard	66	72	57	63	4.9	10.5	3C	3C
34	Trestle Glen, Lakemore, Glenview	82	88	44	47	3.1	4.4	4B	4B
35	Trestle Glen, Lakemore, Glenview	94	96	36	28	4.0	7.9	4B	4B
36	Grand Avenue	89	91	63	62	4.1	7.3	4C	4C
37	Grand Avenue	80	82	58	65	4.6	10.0	4C	4C
38	Central Oakland	69	77	65	67	3.5	5.9	3C	4C
39	Rockridge	90	93	36	34	3.4	4.3	4B	4B
40	Merriewood, Claremont District	79	92	35	23	1.7	3.1	3B	4A
41	Montclair, Forest Park	87	94	31	21	1.6	2.7	4B	4A
42	Montclair, Piedmont Pines ...	84	92	33	20	1.9	4.3	4B	4A

Census Tract	Identifying Place Name	Social Rank 1940	Social Rank 1950	Urbanization 1940	Urbanization 1950	Segregation 1940	Segregation 1950	Social Area 1940	Social Area 1950
43	Laurel	51	68	30	26	3.9	6.2	3B	3B
44	Diamond	59	72	30	26	2.1	4.7	3B	3B
45	Diamond	69	74	39	38	2.9	5.0	3B	3B
46	Twenty-third Avenue	52	64	49	52	6.3	14.3	3B	3C
47	Twenty-third Avenue	49	60	39	36	5.1	11.0	2B	3B
48	Diamond	50	62	36	40	2.6	5.8	3B	3B
49	Allendale	43	55	33	38	3.9	9.5	2B	3B
50	Foothill, Allendale	49	56	39	38	3.4	7.4	2B	3B
51	Foothill, Allendale	46	59	35	42	3.7	7.1	2B	3B
52	Twenty-third Avenue	33	45	48	51	13.7	22.0	2BS	2CS
53	Fruitvale	53	60	59	61	5.4	7.2	3C	3C
54	Fruitvale	48	55	55	55	5.1	7.1	2C	3C
55	Fruitvale	23	31	38	45	15.6	28.3	1BS	2BS
56	Melrose, Fruitvale	19	36	36	35	17.5	15.7	1BS	2B
57	Melrose, Fairfax	47	53	48	49	6.0	11.2	2B	3B
58	Fairfax, Allendale	52	64	36	37	2.7	7.1	3B	3B
59	Fairfax	71	72	34	33	2.7	6.2	3B	3B
60	Leona Heights, Laurel	58	73	31	37	3.2	5.3	3B	3B
61*	Leona Heights, Oakmore	59	72	27	39	2.5	6.6	3B	3B
62	Millsmont, Eastmont	51	69	25	29	2.0	5.3	3B	3B
63	Elmhurst	44	57	29	30	4.8	8.9	2B	3B
64	Seminary	42	54	32	35	5.8	11.7	2B	3B
65	Seminary	45	54	34	37	5.0	10.1	2B	3B
66	Melrose, Elmhurst	24	45	27	25	11.8	28.6	1B	2BS
67	Brookfield	27	53	37	13	22.6	7.0	2BS	3A
68	Elmhurst, Stonehurst	22	43	32	31	16.7	25.0	1BS	2BS
69	Elmhurst	36	47	31	33	7.8	11.3	2B	2B
70	Stonehurst	39	53	26	27	7.6	10.7	2B	3B
71	Eastmont, Castlemont	58	70	22	27	3.0	5.9	3A	3B
72*	Oak Knoll, Sheffield	74	83	22	19	2.8	4.4	3A	4A

Tracts in the City of Berkeley

Census Tract	Identifying Place Name	Social Rank 1940	Social Rank 1950	Urbanization 1940	Urbanization 1950	Segregation 1940	Segregation 1950	Social Area 1940	Social Area 1950
1-A	West Berkeley	26	51	27	33	17.0	53.3	2BS	3BS
1-B	West Berkeley	26	40	39	44	19.9	43.2	2BS	2BS
2-A	South Berkeley	39	52	41	54	41.7	76.6	2BS	3CS
2-B	South Berkeley	46	57	50	59	43.7	83.8	2CS	3CS
2-C	South Berkeley	58	64	47	51	45.3	71.7	3BS	3CS
2-D	South Berkeley	42	51	46	41	34.3	56.6	2BS	3BS
3-A	South Berkeley	58	73	53	53	5.9	13.2	3C	3C
3-B	Elmwood	80	88	61	64	5.4	5.8	4C	4C
3-C	Elmwood	93	94	65	67	2.8	4.6	4C	4C
3-D	Claremont	96	97	56	59	3.4	5.6	4C	4C
3-E	Claremont	101	96	43	33	3.9	6.5	4B	4B
4-A	West of Grove Street	46	62	40	49	11.9	15.3	2B	3B
4-B	West of Grove Street	59	75	53	58	6.0	11.1	3C	4C
4-C	West of Grove Street	69	78	42	46	4.6	8.5	3B	4B
4-D	West of Grove Street	50	66	32	36	8.5	15.1	3B	3B

* One enumeration district in census tract 72 was erroneously tabulated with census tract 61 in 1950. This error in the census bulletin for Oakland was discovered too late for correction in this report.

Census Tract	Identifying Place Name	Social Rank		Urbani-zation		Segre-gation		Social Area	
		1940	1950	1940	1950	1940	1950	1940	1950
4–E	West of Grove Street	52	72	46	50	12.0	17.1	3B	3C
5–A	Shattuck Avenue	78	81	86	81	7.8	12.3	4D	4D
5–B	University of California and environs	96	98	84	83	5.1	7.6	4D	4D
5–C	North Berkeley	100	100	54	50	2.1	4.6	4C	4C
5–D	North Berkeley	85	90	51	57	2.7	5.7	4C	4C
5–E	Shattuck Avenue	83	86	71	76	7.6	8.9	4C	4D
6–A	North Berkeley	93	96	35	24	1.7	4.1	4B	4A
6–B	North Berkeley, Cragmont ...	100	99	41	40	2.0	3.8	4B	4B
6–C	North Berkeley, North Crag-mont	99	103	31	26	2.4	3.7	4B	4B
6–D	North Berkeley, North Crag-mont	99	100	34	27	2.3	3.8	4B	4B
6–E	North Berkeley, Thousand Oaks, North Brae	89	90	30	35	1.7	3.9	4B	4B
Tracts in Adjacent Area									
AC–1	Albany	70	76	25	26	2.6	5.1	3B	4B
AC–2	Albany	73	77	24	34	2.5	4.2	3A	4B
AC–3	Albany	50	60	35	32	5.9	11.8	3B	3B
AC–4	Albany	45	56	25	26	8.0	11.1	2B	3B
AC–5	Albany	43	64	39	41	8.2	37.7	2B	3BS
AC–6	Emeryville	35	43	42	52	10.6	18.4	2B	2C
AC–7	Piedmont	94	96	42	32	4.5	8.1	4B	4B
AC–8	Piedmont	89	90	39	28	3.2	4.4	4B	4B
AC–9	Alameda, Fernside	70	78	30	32	6.0	3.9	3B	4B
AC–10	Alameda	47	51	38	37	15.9	17.6	2BS	3B
AC–11	West Alameda	51	58	37	36	8.0	20.6	3B	3B
AC–12	Alameda	60	71	48	51	5.3	5.5	3B	3C
AC–13	Alameda	76	77	52	55	2.9	4.6	4C	4C
AC–14	Alameda	63	71	56	61	5.4	5.0	3C	3C
AC–15	Alameda	64	72	39	43	3.0	4.2	3B	3B
AC–16	Alameda	57	67	34	32	5.4	7.3	3B	3B
AC–17	San Leandro	50	62	35	27	10.8	12.8	3B	3B
AC–18	San Leandro	66	70	33	32	3.2	6.3	3B	3B
AC–19	San Leandro	29	54	34	39	19.4	20.4	2BS	3B
AC–20	San Leandro		52		14		10.7		3A
CCC–1	Richmond	54	68	28	26	2.8	4.2	3B	3B
CCC–2	Richmond	44	59	30	25	4.8	4.5	2B	3B
CCC–3	Richmond	28	39	34	39	23.6	47.8	2BS	2BS
CCC–4	Richmond	39	49	34	34	9.7	26.3	2B	2BS
CCC–5	Richmond	42	61	34	36	4.9	8.7	2B	3B
CCC–6	Richmond	32	51	29	31	12.1	19.3	2B	3B
CCC–7	Richmond	37	53	45	50	9.6	12.0	2B	3C
CCC–8	Richmond	27	49	23	38	12.5	23.6	2A	2BS
CCC–9	El Cerrito	73	83	26	19	11.6	6.6	3B	4A
CCC–10	El Cerrito	28	53	36	32	17.3	27.0	2BS	3BS
CCC–11	El Cerrito	38	65	30	28	6.3	7.0	2B	3B
CCC–12	El Cerrito	58	79	23	22	3.9	4.9	3A	4A
CCC–13	(Unincorporated)	32	56	31	36	5.2	5.1	2B	3B

APPENDIX B

STANDARDIZATION OF SCORES TO THE RANGES OF THE INDEX COMPONENTS IN LOS ANGELES, 1940

All of the measures composing the indexes of social rank and urbanization have been standardized to their respective ranges in Los Angeles in 1940. Thus, a single scale is established for the direct comparison of census tract scores on the respective indexes for different cities at the same time or the same city at different times. Intracity comparison is not handicapped and intercity comparisons are made possible. Of course, the index of segregation scores are comparable since they are simple percentages. In the 1940 Los Angeles analysis the scores composing the indexes of social rank and urbanization were standardized to a range of 0 to 100 in the following way:

a) The basic formula for standardization:

$$s = x(r - o)$$

where

s = standardized score
o = lower limit of the census tract ratios for each component
r = ratio for a particular census tract
$$x = \frac{100}{\text{range of the ratio}}$$

b) For those variables (occupation, education, fertility, and single-family dwelling units) which had an inverse relation to the basic indexes for which they were computed (social rank and urbanization), the formula was adjusted to read as follows:

$$s = 100 - [x(r - o)]$$

c) The range, the lower limit of the range, and the conversion factor (x) for each of the ratios for the Los Angeles Area, 1940, are as follows:

Ratio	Range	Lower Limit (o)	Conversion Factor (x)
Occupation	748	0	.1336898
Education	770	130	.1298701
Fertility	602	9	.1661130
Women in the labor force	458	86	.2183406
Single-family dwelling units	994	6	.1006441

If the range of a given ratio in another city exceeds the range in Los Angeles in 1940, of course, it is possible to achieve a standard score less than 0 or greater than 100. The procedure followed in the study of the San Francisco Bay Region reported here was to group those tracts falling outside the social space diagram with the nearest social area.

If the application of this method to the census tract data for other metropolitan regions shows that very many census tract populations achieve social rank or urbanization scores less than 0 or in excess of 100, then some other procedure should be used to standardize the index components. The simplest alternative method would be merely to average the actual ratios for the variables composing the index of social rank and the index of urbanization respectively and move the decimal one place to the left. This is consistent with the procedure used in the index of segregation and reduces some of the computation necessary to apply the typology. This procedure would assume that the occupation ratio, the education ratio, the fertility ratio, the women in the labor force ratio, and the single-family dwelling units ratio each had the limits of 0 and 1,000.

For every ratio except the fertility ratio such limits do in fact represent the lowest and highest value that these ratios can take on. For the fertility ratio a lower limit of 0 would be the lowest possible limit the ratio could take on, but the upper limit would be arbitrarily set at 1,000, since the fertility ratio can exceed this value. However, a fertility ratio of 1,000 seems a reasonable upper limit to establish for urban subpopulations.

APPENDIX C

TWO VIEWS OF THE CONSTRUCTS

While we do not have sufficient space here to fully discuss in any detail the implications of the alternative designations for the three constructs—social rank or economic status, urbanization or family status, and segregation or ethnic status—we feel it is necessary to indicate that two slightly different views of the constructs are involved.

This typology is the result of an "ordering" of patterns of variables which we take to be indicants of urban behavior. The three indexes are constructed to indicate "positions" within these ordered patterns. The Social Rank construct permits the setting up of hierarchies determined overvalently by economic elements. The Segregation construct permits the setting up of "hierarchies" of interaction patterns reflecting social values directed toward ethnic and cultural variations. The Urbanization construct is of a much different order. Its referent is largely within the organizational structure of the economic system. This view of urbanization as a social process which has impact on the social interaction patterns should lead us to view the census variables selected for the construction of the urbanization index as *indicants* of structural functional changes at a level transcending the immediate family interaction. This higher conceptual level is more congruous with the perspective held in the social rank and segregation analysis. (Note by Shevky.)

Another view follows: Economic status is suggested for social rank, family status for urbanization, and ethnic status for segregation. Using *status* to refer to each factor emphasizes the fact that each subpopulation's *position* with respect to each dimension or factor is determined. No prestige connotation is implied here by the use of the term "status." *Economic* status is suggested for *social* rank to make more specific the intended connotation of the construct. Family status and ethnic status are also "social" statuses. *Family* status limits the conception of urbanization, but more precisely directs attention to that aspect of urbanization being measured with the index as presently constructed. To say that family status increased for the Bay Region population from 1940 to 1950, for example, represents a generally accepted notion, but to say that the urban Bay Region population decreased in urbanization is difficult to conceive. In addition to emphasizing the concept of "position," the use of the term "ethnic status" rather than "segregation" reduces possible confusion with the index of isolation and the group segregation ratio, which are also a part of this method of analysis. (Note by Bell.)

BIBLIOGRAPHY

1. Beals, Ralph L. "Urbanism, Urbanization and Acculturation," *American Anthropologist*, 53 (January–March, 1951): 1–10.
2. Bell, Wendell. "A Comparative Study in the Methodology of Urban Analysis." Unpublished Ph.D. dissertation, University of California, Los Angeles, 1952.
3. ———. "A Probability Model for the Measurement of Ecological Segregation," *Social Forces*, 32 (May 1954): 357–64.
4. ———. "The Social Areas of the San Francisco Bay Region," *American Sociological Review*, 18 (February 1953): 39–47.
5. Bogue, Donald J. *State Economic Areas*. Washington, D.C.: U.S. Government Printing Office, 1951.
6. Bossard, James H. S., and Winogene Pratt Sanger. "The Large Family System: A Research Report," *American Sociological Review*, 17 (February 1952): 3–9.
7. Broom, Leonard, and Eshref Shevky. "The Differentiation of an Ethnic Group," *American Sociological Review*, 14 (August 1949): 476–81.
8. Burgess, Ernest, and Harvey J. Locke. *The Family*. New York, 1945.
9. Clark, Colin. *The Conditions of Economic Progress*. 2d ed. London, 1951.
10. ———. "The Economic Functions of a City in Relation to its Size," *Econometrica*, 13 (April 1945): 97–113.
11. Fisher, Allan G. B. "Production, Primary, Secondary and Tertiary," *Economic Record*, 15 (1939): 24–38.
12. Fletcher, R. C., H. L. Hornback, and Stuart A. Queen. *Social Statistics of St. Louis by Census Tracts*. St. Louis: Washington University Press, 1935.
13. Florence, P. Sargant. *The Logic of British and American Industry: A Realistic Analysis of Economic Structure and Government*. London, 1953.
14. Goldschmidt, Walter. *As You Sow*. New York, 1947.
15. Goodrich, Carter, *et al*. *Migration and Economic Opportunity; The Report of the Study of Population Redistribution*. Philadelphia: University of Pennsylvania Press, 1936.
16. Grebler, Leo. "Implications of Rent Control, Experience in the United States," *International Labour Review*, 65 (April 1952): 462–81.
17. Green, Arnold W. "The Middle Class Male Child and Neurosis," *American Sociological Review*, 11 (February 1946): 31–41.
18. Greer, Scott. *Social Organization*. New York, 1954.
19. Hagood, Margaret J. "Statistical Methods for Delineation of Regions Applied to Data on Agriculture and Population," *Social Forces*, 21 (March 1943): 288–97.
20. Haig, Robert Murray. "Towards an Understanding of the Metropolis—The Assignment of Activities to Areas in Urban Regions," *Quarterly Journal of Economics*, 40 (1926): 402–34.
21. Hajnal, John. "The Marriage Boom," *Population Index*, 19 (April 1953): 80–94.
22. Harris, Chauncey D. "A Functional Classification of Cities in the United States," *Geographical Review*, 33 (January 1943): 86–89.
23. Jaffe, A. J. "Differential Fertility in the White Population in Early America," *Journal of Heredity*, 31 (September 1940): 407–11.
24. Lotka, Alfred J. *Elements of Physical Biology*. Baltimore, 1925.
25. McKenzie, Roderick D. *The Neighborhood: A Study of Local Life in the City of Columbus, Ohio*. Chicago: University of Chicago Press, 1923.
26. Mills, C. Wright. *White Collar*. New York: Oxford University Press, 1951.
27. Myers, Charles A., and Rupert MacLaurin. *The Movement of Factory Workers: A Study of a New England Industrial Community*. New York, 1943.
28. Notestein, Frank W. "Population—the Long View," in Theodore W. Schultz, *Food for the World*. Chicago: University of Chicago Press, 1945.
29. Ogburn, William F. "The Family and Its Functions," *Recent Social Trends in the United States*, 1 (New York, 1933): 661–79.
30. Park, Robert E., and Herbert A. Miller. *Old World Traits Transplanted*. New York, 1921.
31. Parsons, Talcott. "The Kinship System of the Contemporary United States," *American Anthropologist*, 45 (January–March, 1943): 22–38.

32. Pearl, Raymond. "The Aging of Populations," *Journal of the American Statistical Association*, 35 (1940): 277–97.
33. Pirenne, Henri. *Medieval Cities: Their Origin and the Revival of Trade*. Princeton: Princeton University Press, 1925.
34. Robinson, William S. "Ecological Correlations and the Behavior of Individuals," *American Sociological Review*, 15 (June 1950): 351–57.
35. Salz, Arthur. "Occupation," *Encyclopedia of the Social Sciences*, 6 (New York, 1937): 424–35.
36. Schmid, Calvin F. *Social Saga of Two Cities*. Minneapolis, 1937.
37. ———. *Social Trends in Seattle*. Seattle: University of Washington Press, 1944.
38. Schultz, Theodore W. *The Economic Organization of Agriculture*. New York, 1953.
39. Shevky, Eshref, and Marilyn Williams. *The Social Areas of Los Angeles: Analysis and Typology*. Berkeley and Los Angeles: University of California Press, 1949.
40. Spengler, Joseph J. "Economic Factors in the Development of Densely Populated Areas," *Proceedings of the American Philosophical Society*, 95 (1951): 20–53.
41. Sundbärg, A. G. Institut International de Statistique, *Bulletin*, 12 (1900): 90–95.
42. Thomas, Dorothy Swaine. "Research Memorandum on Migration Differentials," *Social Science Research Council Bulletin*, 43 (1938).
43. Thomas, W. I., and Florian Znaniecki. *The Polish Peasant in Europe and America*. Boston, 1920.
44. Thornthwaite, Charles W. *Internal Migration in the United States*. Philadelphia: University of Pennsylvania Press, 1934.
45. U.S. Bureau of the Census. *Population and Housing, Statistics for Census Tracts, 16th Census of the United States, 1940*. Washington, D.C.: U.S. Government Printing Office.
46. U.S. Bureau of the Census. *United States Census of Population, Census Tract Statistics, 1950*, Vol. III (Series P-D). Washington, D.C.: U.S. Government Printing Office.
47. Vance, Rupert B. *All These People*. Chapel Hill, 1946.
48. Ware, Caroline F. "Ethnic Communities," *Encyclopedia of the Social Sciences*, 3 (New York, 1937): 607–13.
49. Warner, W. Lloyd, and Leo Srole. *The Social System of American Ethnic Groups*. New Haven: Yale University Press, 1945.
50. Wendling, Aubrey. "Suicide in the San Francisco Bay Region 1938–1942 and 1948–1952." Unpublished Ph.D. dissertation, University of Washington, 1954.
51. Wiener, Norbert. *The Human Use of Human Beings*. Boston, 1950.
52. Wilson, Godfrey, and Monica Wilson. *Analysis of Social Change*. London: Cambridge University Press, 1945.
53. Wirth, Louis. "Urbanism as a Way of Life," *American Journal of Sociology*, 44 (July 1938): 1–24.
54. Zorbaugh, Harvey W. *The Gold Coast and the Slum*. Chicago: University of Chicago Press, 1929.